BAKE SALES
are my
B*TCH

Aug 2019

BAKE SALES
are my
B*TCH

Win the Food Allergy Wars with
60+ Recipes
to Keep Kids Safe and
Parents Sane

April Peveteaux

RODALE.

RODALE *wellness*

Live happy. Be healthy. Get inspired.

Sign up today to get exclusive access to our authors, exclusive bonuses,
and the most authoritative, useful, and cutting-edge information on health,
wellness, fitness, and living your life to the fullest.

Visit us online at RodaleWellness.com
Join us at RodaleWellness.com/Join

© 2016 by April Peveteaux

Rodale books may be purchased for business or promotional use or for special sales.
For information, please write to:
Special Markets Department, Rodale Inc., 733 Third Avenue, New York, NY 10017

Printed in the United States of America
Rodale Inc. makes every effort to use acid-free ♾, recycled paper ♲.

Book design by Carol Angstadt

Library of Congress Cataloging-in-Publication Data is on file with the publisher.
ISBN 978–1–62336–720–6   paperback

Distributed to the trade by Macmillan
2   4   6   8   10   9   7   5   3   1   paperback

Follow us @RodaleBooks on 🐦 📘 📌 📷

We inspire health, healing, happiness, and love in the world.
Starting with you.

Dedicated to the vigilant,
yet terrified,
parents of allergic kids
everywhere

Contents

Introduction

Hello, everyone in the world! At least that's who I am assuming is reading this introduction to *Bake Sales Are My B*tch*. Because we're all suffering here—parents, kids, teachers, the lunch lady, chefs, wait staff, and especially those poor grandparents who "just know" that soy allergies are a bunch of hooey. I'm sorry to report this to those of you who wish to put this book back on the shelf and never think about kids and food issues ever again, but no one is untouched by the dramatic increase in food allergies among our children. You may think that you won the genetic lottery because *your* kids not only don't have any allergies at all but also are in the 90th percentile in height, answer "kale" every time you ask what they want for dinner, and are already developing a six-pack in the 3rd grade. Sorry, supermom or -dad (or both— really you *both* should be reading this), you can't escape from the great food allergy/intolerance/preference/unidentified food issues of the 21st century. NO ONE CAN.

Listen up, moms and dads, there are as many food allergies and preferences in any given school as there are nits, that's a fact. Okay, that's not a fact, and there are probably more nits, but I don't want to gross you out as we talk about food. But a female head louse does lay about 88 nits during her short lifetime. So they're all up in there. Sorry, I totally just grossed you out after saying I didn't want to. Damn it! The point is, whether you have an allergic kid or not, at some point, you will be required (or asked, most likely) to consider leaving out a key ingredient to your world-famous chocolate pecan shortbread. No matter how much you wish that were not so, the fact is 1 out of every 25 children in the United States suffers from food allergies, and those numbers are growing rapidly, with a 50 percent increase between 1997 and 2011.[1] That's a lot of kids with food problems, and since 88 percent of schools report having one or more children with food allergies,[2] it's going to be all up in your kid's lunch box soon enough. Let's talk about how to get through that tough time without making yourself insane trying to create the perfect dairy-free copy of cream cheese ice cream or, the alternative, coming off like the world's biggest asshole when you declare, "In my day, food allergies weeded out the weak!"

Unless you're homeschooling your perfectly developing child in a bubble that does not allow for anyone outside its sphere to enter the inner sanctum, there will always be a miniature adult hanging out next to your kid in the lunchroom, at birthday parties, at classroom celebrations, and even in your own home who cannot tolerate some kind of food something or other. For those of us parents of children with unsullied immune systems (for now—we all know people who develop problems with food well into adulthood), it can be crazy-making to pack a peanut-free, tree-nut-free, dairy-free, gluten-free lunch 5 days a week. I get to add "kosher" to my list of grade-schooler lunch requirements, and I know loads of people who also tag on "vegan" when they're preparing food for their kids, because, clearly, they are sadists. Throwing a 5-year-old birthday party becomes a land mine of requests/requirements and, many times, we may be tempted to just call bullshit in the face of another "please make it refined-sugar-free" text. (Pro tip: That's what the middle finger emoji is for.)

I can hear you getting overwhelmed as you read this. I was overwhelmed as I wrote this, but probably for different reasons. It's true that you cannot feed all of the people all of the time. I actually saw a Yelp review where the diner explained he/she was allergic to "mammalian meat," and I don't think *anyone* knows what to do with that one. So, here's what I am going to do to make it (somewhat) simple. I'm going to focus on the eight foods that account for 90 percent of allergic reactions: dairy, eggs, wheat/gluten, peanuts, tree nuts, soy, shellfish, and fish. Given my own lunch box situation with my kids, I'm also going to touch a bit on vegan, kosher, and other dietary restrictions as well. I mean, why not just go for it, right? I'm here to provide recipes and, hopefully, some kind of comfort for parents who are trying to keep their allergic kid safe, while teaching the rest of the world how to be a more accommodating place for these kids and their completely freaked-out parents. As a proud member of the freaked-out parent club, I, too, have had brushes with minor allergies with my daughter. As someone who has celiac disease, I'm also always looking for signs of celiac in my own kids and always forcing them to test my gluten-free cupcakes. But only one of those things is truly stress inducing. To me. My kids only run away one out of three times when I call out from the kitchen, "No, really! These are the GOOD cupcakes." I may already have an extra sensitivity to food issues, but it doesn't mean that I'm not capable of completely losing it if a pediatrician tells me to remove one more food from our family's diet. I am, and you know I will if that one food happens to be dairy.

While it can certainly appear that there are two distinct sides to the great food allergy debate—those with issues, and those without—the fact is, we are all in this together. In America, we often hear the refrain "not my problem" anytime someone asks for a little assistance—be it with early airline boarding for a family with three wildcatting toddlers or obtaining affordable health care. Unfortunately, that refrain consistently bleeds into our conversations about children and food because we're special that way. From the mom who demanded our preschool no-peanuts rule be changed because her 4-year-old "only eats peanut butter sandwiches" to the regularity of food allergy fights breaking out online, it's clear that those with allergic children are constantly battling negative perceptions; and those who think allergies are bullshit can seem to be more concerned with little Caleb's snack options than causing death or illness to another kiddo. Oh, you don't believe adults actually behave in that manner? Not one, but two parents have sued schools after a peanut butter ban went into effect due to severe allergies of other students. One parent sued the school because she claimed that her daughter would not be getting her nutritional needs met,[3] and another because it violated her 5-year-old's rights as her child had been enjoying peanut butter sandwiches all summer.[4] Sure, seems legit. And let me just throw in one recent example that found its way to my Facebook feed. Of course, it had to do with Halloween. OF COURSE.

Scary Mommy is a real-life successful "mom blog" that gets a zillion page views and probably makes millions for all involved (just kidding, we all know moms are only allowed to make "latte money" even when we're actually the women changing the way society looks at every damn issue from equal pay to domestic abuse). You're going to find your contentious parenting issues on this site, just like you do in so many other parenting publications, because mom fights sell Pampers. And wine, if my Facebook ads are to be believed.

It was not at all difficult for me to stumble upon a blog post entitled, "Over-the-Top Allergy Parent Shames Neighborhood for Their Halloween Candy Offerings[5]" just in time for the holidays! The *Scary Mommy* blogger took issue with a parent's notice put up around the neighborhood asking her neighbors to please consider her very allergic kid. Here's the text of the sign, which we should note WAS in ALL CAPS (except for the treat suggestions, where it is assumed the parent chilled):

ATTENTION PARENTS

MY SON HAS SEVERE ALLERGIES AND COMES HOME DEVASTATED EVERY YEAR THAT HE CAN'T EAT ANY CANDY THAT HE HAS COLLECTED AT YOUR HOMES WHILE TRICK-OR-TREATING. DON'T EXCLUDE MY CHILD, OR ANY OTHER CHILD FROM THE FUN.

THIS HALLOWEEN, PRACTICE RESPONSIBLE PARENTING AND DO NOT DISTRIBUTE CANDY WITH NUTS OF ANY KIND, GLUTEN, OR DAIRY.

BE MINDFUL OF EVERYONE'S CHILD—HERE ARE SOME TASTY AND ALLERGY-CONSCIOUS SUGGESTIONS:

Carrot sticks
(fun to eat, healthy, and easy on the teeth)

Smarties

Necco Wafers

Life Savers

Brach's Lemon Drops

Raisins (but stay away from Raisinets!!!!!!!)

Personally, I don't know why this wasn't in an email missive, but way to kick it old school in the neighborhood, allergy mom/dad!

Depending on who you are, you may disagree on who is being the douche rocket here—the people who attack this (assumed-to-be) mom or the person posting this message all over the neighborhood. While your initial reaction may be like the *Scary Mommy* blogger, as you toss out a "how dare she ruin Halloween for the children?!" maybe think again.

This ALL CAPS declaration may not be the way I would handle Halloween if I had an allergic kid dressing up and begging for sugar, and clearly other parents of allergic kids choose different ways to protect their kids during the treat season that aren't so yell-y. I'm guessing they also get better results. Still, so many people in the *Scary Mommy* comments section (which, oh boy, don't start reading if you don't want to see how dark humanity can get) are calling her "paranoid," "entitled," "crazy" and "lazy." I think we should explore some of these accusations and defend this parent before the pile-on gets even bigger and uglier, if that's at all possible.

First of all, haters, of course she's paranoid and crazy—*her kid could die* if he eats Halloween candy! How sane can you be knowing that your child's life is at risk every time he walks outside of your home? How many tears do you think this parent has cried as she canceled another playdate or birthday party because she'd rather not have her child go to the hospital on such a lovely Saturday? "Entitled" is also a shitty one because, seriously, what is she feeling entitled to? Oh, right, HER CHILD NOT DYING. I kind of feel entitled to that not happening on major holidays as well. Call me selfish. Some of you already have, so that was probably not necessary. But I believe we do have to take issue with "lazy" because that note took all kinds of energy and effort. Bravo, note lady. Or note man. I guess we don't actually know who did this, but let's pretend it's a mom because IT'S SO GREAT TO BASH MOMS.[6]

While you and I may handle Halloween, and life, quite differently than the candy parent, when someone has a child with a serious life-threatening health issue and is reaching out for help, we don't get to decide how she asks. Sure, we should all be respectful and not be unhinged in our dealings with our fellow humans, but that's not always how your day goes, you know?

Still.

If someone in our community needs our help, why can't we offer it without judgment? Or, move along if we don't have time or the mental bandwidth, and still not trash-talk the askee all around town. Or, at least save our judgment for our alone time with our partners who know how we really feel about the neighbor with no fence around her pool. No need to write a blog post shaming a mom, even if you think she's the one shaming an entire neighborhood. We're all in this parenting game together, and we need to focus on our commonalities, not our differences. Because what we all have in common is that we're just really tired of making kid food, and exhaustion makes us cranky.

That's all I'm trying to do here—get us all to imagine life from the other parent's perspective. Practice a little empathy while keeping our kiddos safe. And there's nothing that says we can't keep our own children safe and healthy while also considering other busy moms' limitations. Working together is challenging, sure, but if we can all put ourselves in some other gal's slip-ons, we'll all be happier, less stressed, and much more filled with kindness and light and gluten-free cookies. So, yeah, we're going to learn how to make party foods that are the mother scratchin' bomb and serve them up to everyone with a genuine smile—even that lady who believes peanut allergies are all in your head. Let's do this.

Chapter

①

Fuck, My Kid Is Sick

ongratulations! It's an allergic baby boy! I mean, they don't actually say that in the delivery room, but a heck of a lot of parents are hearing it shortly after they arrive home and discover that breast milk after drinking a milkshake means violent diarrhea and projectile vomiting from the little bundle of joy. The gluten allergy rears its ugly head right around the time you introduce solids, or the peanut problem shows up when your toddler gets her hands on the Jif jar for the first time. There are a million different ways to discover a food allergy in your kids, all of them unpleasant. And as food allergies increase among our children, we're in for a lot more unpleasantness. Putting the debate aside about whether it's our "messed with" food or more awareness that's causing this uptick in food allergies, let's deal head-on with the task at hand, which is figuring out what's going on with your little hive-covered pooper and how to make it stop. How, you may ask, does one even find out about childhood food allergies? No, the answer is not the Internet. Of course, it can be. But let's start at the doctor's office, m'kay?

Once you become a parent, you have one job: Keep that baby alive. Okay, there's more to it than that, but that is kind of the biggie. I know that I lay awake listening for breathing when my firstborn started sleeping through the night, meaning, no, I never really slept through the night, even as my baby did. Becoming a parent is absolutely amazing in its terrifyingness. You have this beautiful (yes, even old-man-looking babies), precious, tiny little bundle, and she's ENTIRELY VULNERABLE. God, it's awful.

While one does eventually stop checking for nocturnal breathing (I think that happens somewhere around 13, but then you start checking for the aroma of weed), there are so many other real or perceived dangers out there just waiting to clothesline the most special people in our lives. Or at least that's how it can feel when you're a neurotic (read normal) parent in the 21st century. Food allergies being one of the most annoying and frightening dangers, depending on the hand you've been dealt.

All parents have been up late with a vomiting toddler, cleaning up and making sure he's lying on his side. And who hasn't lost a month or more of productivity thanks to the annual family respiratory virus? As parents, we're used to dealing with sick kids, and no matter how horrible it may be in the moment, we know it, too, will pass. Additionally, those limited times of being sick are helped by pediatrician visits that reassure us that no, it's not typhoid fever, and yes, she will be back in school in time for her starring role in *Peter Pan*. This is our normal, and we've got this. Or at least we eventually get it, after several months of panicking every time our baby looks at us weird.

Any chronic illness or condition, however, will kick our collective parenting butts. Especially because there comes a time when we're not allowed to hang out in the pediatrician's office all day, every day, even if our child does have to deal with the nasty effects of a food allergy, all day, every day. Once your baby hits a certain milestone, you're kind of on your own for the day-to-day business of "Why does she sound like that? Is that an infection?" which may be the reason why food allergies are most common in babies and small children. Doctor visits are more common than date nights, which may also be why sometimes we might be crushing on that pediatrician.

The good, and completely exhausting, thing when you have a newborn is that you're at the doctor's office all the time. No new reaction to her environment, eating pattern, or issue goes unsaid. When you're in the early days and months, babies are monitored as if they'd joined their local Scientology sect.

This is actually incredibly helpful for new parents, and new human beings who may need some extra care while developing those gross motor skills. You should always walk into a pediatrician visit prepared to talk about any changes in diet, in reaction, in bathroom habits, in fussiness, or anything at all that strikes you, just to make sure that you're on top of what's normal for your baby. And a great pediatrician will prod you for answers even if you're not walking in with a PowerPoint presentation on your baby's 6-month milestones. It's easier to care for your baby with this kind of support, and any deviation from the path will be noted. This is the time when you are paying so much attention to what goes into your baby, and what comes out—especially when it happens after a meal. While not every blob of spit-up or noxious wet poop means food allergies, it is important to monitor what's the usual pattern for your babe . . . and what seems out of the ordinary. Yes, early child care is romantic; why do you ask?

Babies get trickier when you hit that 1-year mark and, suddenly, you're not in your pediatrician's office every month. It can be panic-inducing to not have feedback about your baby on a regular basis, so it's on you to start looking for any signs, if you suspect that your little one has a food allergy. You should still walk into your appointments with a list of concerns to discuss. To be sure, not every negative baby face is an allergic reaction. In fact, most are not. But, if you suspect that food is not your little nugget's friend, be sure to talk to your pediatrician if any of the following seems to be happening on a regular basis.

Possible Signs That Your Kid Is Allergic

1. Fussiness, especially after eating. If your child is suddenly irritated after a meal, it may be gas, or it may be a gas-inducing food allergy.

2. Refusal to nurse or eat. This could be teething or any number of things, but if it continues, you need to get to the bottom of the issue.

3. Rash, hives, or itchiness around the mouth or the butt. There's diaper rash, and then there're allergies. Talk to your doctor if a medicated cream does not clear up the bumps. Any itchiness around the mouth should be checked out immediately.

4. Excessive pooping or blood in the diaper.

5. Wheezing or difficulty breathing.

When your children are older, these are still signs to be aware of after your child has had a meal. Other signs to look for could include anxiety around food or about having a bathroom nearby. A disproportionate swelling of the belly could be a sign of gastrointestinal distress. Extreme fatigue, slow growth, crankiness, and general lethargy should also be checked out. Really anything that is "off" should be brought up to your pediatrician. Use your mom/dad instinct, and don't ignore a persistent issue.

If You Read Nothing Else, Please Read This

Now that I have your attention with all that fun body fluid talk, let's tackle the most frightening and horrific reality of food allergies right away—anaphylaxis. This is the main reason I want to educate parents, caregivers, and friends of the nonallergic and politely guide them to the allergen-free recipe section of this book.

As someone who has absolutely not had my own gluten-freeness taken seriously at times, I can understand how it's confusing to people who don't know what gluten is but are pretty sure it's a Kardashian thing. I may have the luxury of being slipped some gluten and still surviving (by luxury, I mean only pooping my pants), but those who have severe allergic reactions do not. And that is what must be heard above all the "trendy" labels and name-calling that can happen on and off the playground. Food allergies can kill. No ifs, ands, or buts. While, sure, there is something funny about me admitting to that pants-pooping thing, there is nothing at all funny about anaphylaxis. Let's talk about it, learn about it, and never forget it.

While we often hear about children, and even adults, dying from exposure to peanuts, any food allergy can cause anaphylaxis. Some other nonfood allergens can as well, but we're going to focus on food and the safety of our children. The most common foods that do induce this potentially fatal reaction include peanuts, tree nuts, fish, and shellfish. I also personally know of a child with a life-threatening dairy allergy. Anaphylaxis can be caused by any food, and it's terrifying.

Obviously, not every food allergy can lead to such a severe reaction, but unless you've been told otherwise, if you have a child in your care with a food allergy, proceed as if the worst could happen. This is the worst.

Anaphylaxis occurs within minutes, sometimes much longer, after exposure to an allergen. If medical care is not administered within 30 minutes or less, anaphylaxis could lead to death. Some signs that anaphylaxis is occurring include shortness of breath and difficulty breathing, hives or other rash, swelling around the mouth or nose, a weak pulse (which indicates a reduction in blood pressure), confusion, fainting, vomiting, diarrhea, or other gastrointestinal symptoms. A child with asthma in addition to a food allergy is more likely to have difficulty breathing to the point of death. A shot of epinephrine right away is the first course of action when someone is suffering an anaphylactic reaction, followed immediately by a call to 911.

Talk to your pediatrician about always having an auto-injector with epinephrine on hand. You should carry one, as well as any other caregiver who is with your child. Your child's school should have more than one ready and available, and if your child is old enough to carry one himself, he should be well versed in how to use it and what to do next. Always make sure that you have at least two epinephrine injectors on hand at all times, and your injector is up-to-date, as they do expire after 1 year. But even if you only have an expired epinephrine shot, the Food Allergy Research and Education (FARE)[1] organization recommends that you use it and call 911 immediately.

Sometimes you find out that your child's allergic reaction is more severe than you had realized. Previously your kiddo had a bum tummy, but now some itching around the mouth has presented itself when she came home from Grandma's house. Even without the presence of asthma or anaphylaxis, most pediatricians and allergists will prescribe an EpiPen or other auto-injector of epinephrine. I have one even though my seasonal allergies and celiac disease are two very separate things. A cautious doctor is a good thing, especially when it comes to the safety of your children. Be sure you ask your child's doctor about the necessity of having an auto-injector available to your child, and learn how to use it properly and safely. While avoiding the allergen at all costs is the first line of defense, the second, and very successful, line of defense for dealing with severe food allergies is this auto-injector of epinephrine. If you act quickly and follow up in the hospital, your child can remain safe. You, however, will most likely remain terrified. Sorry.

I almost forgot to tell you the good news about severe allergic reactions: You get jewelry! Or, at least this is how you will explain having to wear a medical bracelet, necklace, or other accoutrement to your tween. While a baby, toddler, or preschooler will rarely be out of range of a caregiver who is fully versed on her health challenges, once your kids get older, they like to go to the mall and things. If your child has an allergic reaction and no one who knows her is around to identify what's happening, it could be disastrous. Having a medical ID bracelet or other type of jewelry that explains her allergy can be lifesaving. Make sure your kiddo is wearing it at all times, and you'll at least feel safer about that thing she's doing on Friday night.

It's Gonna Take Money

For another bad news/good news take on living with a food allergy, let's talk about the financial impact on your family. Any chronic medical condition means the bills begin to add up. From regular doctor visits (which does not include parking costs, gas costs, etc.) to medication that suddenly quadrupled in price to hospital visits to special foods, it is expensive living with a food allergy or sensitivity. The only good news in this scenario is that you can write these expenses off on your taxes in the United States. Sometimes, they will be considered medical expenses, and other times, they could be research, or in the case of a special allergy-friendly sleep-away camp, child care. Talk with your accountant or check out the tax season articles in allergy periodicals (see Resources on page 197) to get the specifics, and don't forget to save those receipts!

What Happens Next?

So, now you suspect something shady is going on with nightshades (see how I did that?). How does one find out, officially, about food allergies? Many of you knew your child had a food allergy based on observation. Sophie ate strawberries and her lips swelled up immediately after. Yep, that's an allergic reaction! At the same time, you really need to confirm your suspicions by seeing a physician. Mom instinct is fierce, but we're talking about the safety of your child, so get it all checked out. One of the first methods an allergist will use to determine if your child has allergies is a skin prick test. While a skin test is a less-definitive test for food allergies, it will alert your physician as to which allergens trigger IgE antibodies, which show an allergic reaction. Since a skin prick is not the same as digesting food, a significant number of false positives do occur with a skin prick test. The skin prick test is more commonly used for environmental and not food allergies, but it still may be part of your repertoire, especially if you already feel like you get sick when you eat citrus, and the test confirms it. I learned that I was allergic to wheat via a skin test after my celiac diagnosis. Not that it changed a dang thing about my life, but obviously every part of my body was trying to tell me to avoid those amber waves of grain. A blood test for the presence of IgE antibodies works in a similar manner, with the main difference being that you don't have to go off of antihistamines before this test, and the results are not as immediate as the skin prick test. The same rates of false positives exist with the blood test as in the skin test. A good doctor will look everywhere for results for your child, and you should be open to getting the most precise answers when it comes to food sensitivities and allergies.

The next step in identifying food allergies is incredibly simple, yet painful. Yes, I'm talking about the elimination diet. Taking every food out of your child's diet is horrible, but it may be the only way you can discover if it's the casein, the main protein in milk, or the lactose that causes your baby to projectile vomit. Fun fact: If you're a nursing mom and your baby is having issues, YOU get to do the elimination diet. Motherhood is so beautiful.

If you're not familiar with the elimination diet, it's basically what it sounds like: eliminating every food that is a potential allergen, and every last bit of joy, out of your child's diet. Your doctor will have an official schedule, but it basically goes like this.

Week 1 Eliminate every suspected food from your child's diet.

Week 2 If your child is feeling better, clearly something in that diet is the culprit. Begin by adding one of the foods back into your child's diet, and check for results.

Week 3 If there is more than one food on the elimination list, you will now add in the other foods one at a time (schedule dependent on the number of foods and the doctor's plan) and check for a reaction. If there is only one, you should have an answer in Week 2.

Week 4 If you have even more foods on the eliminated list, this is the time you'll add the rest in, one at a time, checking for a reaction. Hopefully, this will be the last week that you'll have to do this and the food culprit will be found.

The idea being at the end of this time period, you will have been able to identify which food is most harmful to your child's body, ideally through something less dramatic than a severe allergic reaction. But that could happen, too. Be ready for an emergency once you start introducing foods back into your child's diet, or head into the doctor's office for what is, most of the time, the last step in the allergy discovery process.

If you have identified the allergen, you may want your child to go for the gold standard—the double-blind placebo-controlled food challenge. The double-blind placebo-controlled food challenge takes place in a doctor's office or clinic where your child will be continually monitored. In very simple terms, the patient will be introduced to a food in small doses and observed for any allergic reaction. The doctor and the patient are unaware if the patient is receiving the allergen or a placebo to thwart any bias in the doctor and any anxiety in the patient. If anxiety and bias are not an issue, the oral food challenge will only consist of the allergen. Sounds like a gas, right? Talk to your doctor about the necessity of this food challenge, as it is a way to not only test the specific allergen but also its severity. It may be something you want to do immediately, but not necessarily if you're confident that the allergen has been found. While the food is administered in a medical facility, under the watchful eye of a physician, it still can be scary for your child if he begins to have a severe reaction to the allergen. When your child gets older, the food challenge may be necessary to determine if your child has outgrown his reaction.

While I do know loads of people who, for financial or other reasons, skipped the doctor visit and went straight to eschewing the offending food, I highly recommend that you do not do the same. Your child's gluten reaction could be an autoimmune disease that requires separate treatment. And the dairy issue could be an ulcer. It never pays to self-diagnose or to diagnose your child based on Google searches.

I know it can be frustrating to trot your offspring in and out of a doctor's office and get zero results. It's a special kind of hell to procure an appointment 4 to 6 weeks in the future, get stuck in traffic, and show up 10 minutes late only to have the receptionist inform you that you will now go to the bottom of the list, and then you probably won't get in for another hour, which is just great for your child's nap and/or snack time, and then you get zero results. And you'd better hope your insurance covers it, because probably not so much. Repeat. So many of you have been there, and, eventually, you find something that works in spite of, not because of, what your pediatrician said. I'm super sorry, but it's still worth going through the rigmarole of pediatrician visits, followed by allergists, nutritionists, gastroenterologists, dermatologists, internists, endocrinologists, or any other doctor who could find out what's making your little one itch.

To wrap up this convo about everything horrible, I cannot emphasize this enough: Talk to your pediatrician and make sure that you are 100 percent up to speed on how to handle an anaphylactic reaction if your child is susceptible. Even if your child has not yet presented in any way to make you assume anaphylaxis will occur, be prepared in case the allergy progresses. Review this information with other caregivers, teachers, grandparents, siblings, and parents of your child's friends—anyone who will be around your child.

I Need More!!!

If your child is facing life-threatening food allergies, you will also want to look around for support in the food allergy community. You'll want to stay up-to-date on any new developments in food allergy news, products, treatments, summer camps, and anything else that will make the going a little bit easier. Reaching out to people in the same boat helps to steady your own, so check out FARE (Food Allergy Research and Education), and other groups you will find in the resources section of this book (see page 197). One word of warning: While you'll want to commiserate, plan, and high-five with other parents who are dealing with food allergies, remember, the Internet can lie. Don't take any nutritional advice from a nonprofessional no matter how delicious her acai smoothies look, unless it's been verified by a professional. That's what your doctor, or your actual nutritionist, is for.

Living with an Allergy

Whether your child has a mild reaction to eggs or the worst possible reaction to tree nuts, the moment a parent hears "allergy," she's screaming out every question in the world that basically translates to, "How can I make sure my child doesn't die when he's out of my sight?" This is but one of the challenges of raising a child in the modern world filled with gluten, nuts, and dairy. It's the biggest one, of course, and one no parent leaves the doctor's office without thoroughly understanding. After you've learned all about the allergy, the prevention, the Benadryl, and the epinephrine, it's time to let your kid out into the world. Yes, you can go with him for a time. You probably actually won't let him out of your sight if it's at all possible, at least for a while. Because what comes next can be trickier.

When a child doesn't feel good, the entire house can go under. Teaching an allergic kid to be self-sufficient will be crucial to her health and personal development, and you will be doing that as part of the process of teaching your child about her allergy. Some children will be motivated enough by how they feel to be careful of what they consume, whether a guardian is nearby or not. But some kids will have a tough time speaking up for themselves in the lunchroom or at a sleepover, and that's natural, too. You, of course, will be calling ahead to any location that will be feeding your allergic child. At the same time, she needs to know how to fend for herself since you will not always be with her, say like when the field trip winds up at the ice cream parlor. It will be much easier for the shy kid or the dreamy kid to take care of herself when you're not around, if she knows exactly what to say. Here's a script you can give to your child who is old enough to verbally communicate her needs.

- I have a (nut/dairy/gluten/soy/fish/shellfish/egg) allergy and cannot have that food, or any food with those ingredients. I will get dangerously sick.

- Can you tell me every ingredient in this sandwich/piece of pie/soup?

- Did this food come in contact with (nuts/dairy/gluten/soy/fish/shellfish/eggs)?

Keep it short, simple, and only as detailed as necessary. For example, if you're talking gluten, you're going to have to teach your child all about gluten and where it can be found (see Chapter 3). The same goes for soy, eggs, and dairy. The other of the eight allergens are much more straightforward, but can still be sneaky, so you need to stress the need for your child to ask about every ingredient in the food he is being offered.

While you're teaching your kid to stand on his own and be heard, there will be moments when you have to throw in the towel and let him be a baby again. Even the most mature kids are still not fully developed emotionally or intellectually, no matter how many SAT words they may already know. It's easy to overestimate kids who seem confident and able to take care of themselves, but no kid is perfect, and mistakes will happen. It's not easy living with a food allergy, especially if you accidentally ate the dairy-filled FroYo when you were going for the dairy-free version. Being sick and being functional is incredibly difficult for kids, sometimes impossible. Hey, I'm an adult who is having a tough time sitting in front of a laptop and writing a book I'm getting paid cash money for because I got glutened and have been pooping fire for 2 weeks. How do you expect an 8-year-old to have the energy for Everyday Math homework, if the same is happening to her? Sometimes, you just have to shut it down, put her in bed with a big glass of water, and lie down next to her. There is no shame in surrendering to the bed. None.

How to Talk to Your Child's Teachers and Caretakers

With the numbers of the allergic growing, chances are that your child won't be the first one to educate the fine people who will be responsible for her well-being during school hours. At the same time, you do want to act like it's the first time teachers and caretakers are hearing this, because as far as your child's specific needs go, it is. In addition to explaining, in great detail, what your child's allergies consist of, I implore you to head to the Food Allergy Research and Education website and download the Food Allergy and Anaphylaxis Emergency Care Plan[2] immediately. Print out several copies and distribute them to anyone who is caring for your child. Be sure you include the photo as daycare shifts can change, and substitute teachers are always on call.

Once your child enrolls in school, your first stop should be at the school nurse's office. Making sure the school nurse is informed about your child's medical needs and how to handle an emergency may seem obvious, but this bears repeating. Additionally, the nurse's office will have an extra EpiPen that your child brings to school. Before school even begins, contact the principal and ask for advance meetings with him, the school nurse, your child's teacher, and the lunchroom staff if you're allowing your child to eat their food. Everyone should receive a copy of the emergency care plan, and you should allot time to go over it verbally and answer any questions. This is the time to get the whole team on your side and engaged about your child's health. You want commitment from the people caring for your child, and thorough, respectful communication will go a long way. Even if your child does not experience anaphylaxis, you must educate everyone in a similar thorough manner. No matter how annoying this may sound (and I realize to some of you, making sure your child is taken care of is not annoying in the least), you have to hand out the paperwork, tell each person everything that is on the paperwork, and do it in a calm, kind way to ensure that the listener is open to receiving this information. Don't walk in with the assumption that your 1st grader's teacher is angling to harm your child as soon as you leave the room. Give all of the information while working under the assumption that your child's teachers are part of your team, and that team wants nothing more than to keep your child safe. Of course, if for any reason you do get hostile feedback, you need to talk to your teacher's supervisor, and have your child removed from the classroom, if necessary. This rarely happens as most teachers actually like, and respect, children.

If your child does risk anaphylaxis if he comes into contact with his allergen, you also have to deal with the entire school community. Luckily, there are regulations in place that mean you will receive the support of your public school in the event that your child faces a deadly food allergy. A 504 plan is a written document completed by both the family (the student also participates, which is incredibly helpful in helping her become self-sufficient and safe) and school staff that outlines the allergy and health issues the student is dealing with and how to care for the student in the event of exposure. In addition, the document outlines safety measures that should be in place in the classrooms and common areas where the student will be present, which may be new now that a highly allergic student is attending the school. The school will be responsible for notifying the parents of classmates, teammates, lunch mates, and whomever else comes into contact with the student about the allergy, as well as requesting that no allergens are brought to school or to after-school activities where the child will be present. Your 504 plan will be unique to your family, but some other options include requesting the school send out bullying guidelines related to food allergies or requiring that at least one adult who is capable of using an EpiPen be on-site at all times. It is the plan you all agree to that is designed to keep your child safe while at school and after school. Everything will be communicated in this document, and it will go a long way in making you, the parent, feel like you've been heard.

Okay, then! For all of you who don't have kids with food allergies, are you taking all this gluten-free, dairy-free, soy-free, egg-free, nut-free cookie biz seriously yet? I hope so. Now, let's move on and figure out how to make this all work in this big old playground we call parenting.

Fuck, All My Kid's Friends Are Sick

Congratulations, your house has not been hit with the allergy stick! But as a parent in the world, your kids are bringing home friends for dinner who have serious or mild issues, and you have no idea what to do. Perhaps you're the butter queen at the annual cakewalk and have just recently been informed of a severe milk allergy in your 4th grader's class. Or, maybe you are just a mom or dad who cares about people outside of your own four walls. You rock. Thanks for coming; I'm here to help.

I know I scared everyone proper with the anaphylaxis discussion, and you're welcome. Now is the time to emphasize that even a mild allergic reaction is nothing to sneeze at. An allergic reaction is an autoimmune response wherein your body identifies something (the allergen) as the enemy and begins to attack itself. The result can be mild, such as a little itchiness or stomach upset, or severe, as we discussed with asthma and anaphylaxis. Even if your child's BFF is not prone to severe reactions, the mild reactions are still no walk in the park. And, if a child is repeatedly exposed to the offending allergen, he may develop more severe responses and cause permanent damage to his body.

What I'm saying is that while you may not need to hold an EpiPen throughout dinner with your daughter's soy allergic classmate, you still need to take care with her meal and not serve up the offending food. I highly recommend a thorough discussion with the parent of the allergic child so you are 100 percent clear on the situation, followed by a reading of this book (especially Chapter 2 and all the recipes) so you will be prepared no matter what kid shows up at your dinner table. And they will. Oh, they will.

By creating a safe meal or a safe treat in a safe environment, you are providing an incredibly valuable service for not only the mental health of our children but also, even more dramatically, the physical health of our children. Sure, it's not fun for me to get sick, and the long-term effects are harsh. But I'm an adult and not as vulnerable as a child. Also, I have celiac disease, which, while horrible, is not an immediately life-threatening situation.

Let's break it down: What happens to kids, depending on the severity, is that they can begin to itch, throw up, have intense gastrointestinal pain, or suffer anaphylactic shock and die.

Hence, the importance of taking every care with food you're preparing for the allergic kiddo. You must think about every surface the meal is prepared upon, every ingredient, and everything that happens to that treat on its way into a hungry kid's mouth. Don't be that person that half-assed the allergy-friendly treats at the bake sale or serves PB&J at a playdate. Be a bake-sale sandwich-making hero instead. And then you can put that on your resumé, sister! No, really, do it, and help elevate the status of work done inside the home. Fight it, moms and dads. Fight it.

Multiplication and Division: Allergy Version

Say your child has a milk allergy, which can be just as serious as those pesky nuts, but you have her lunch on lockdown. Congratulations, you are a rock-star mom. Guess what? It's her birthday, and you're stoked to trot out her favorite birthday pie, which just happens to be dairy-free. Again, that's a rock-star move. But wait, it has gluten, which may have a special place in your own dairy-free home, but not in your daughter's BFF's diet. And don't forget about the tree-nut kid, because there is always a tree-nut kid. And dammit, that tree-nut kid needs to be taken seriously, even if society, in general, throws stones. Nuts are nuts, people. Don't discriminate.

As someone who is fighting a war on gluten, I can still find it difficult to accommodate other people's food requirements. It's normal to become fixated on the one offending food in your household and not consider others. But even the allergic are not immune to the other allergic people who surround us at every kid event we find ourselves attending. You may be used to calling up the playdate host and explaining your daughter's dairy allergy, but she may also be used to being the caller due to a peanut situation. Things can get complicated in this modern world, and those of us who already have our own problems should be prepared to welcome in those who will complicate our party menus. As it will be worth it to please every guest who is in need. My favorite dinner parties have been when someone took the initiative to make some naturally gluten-free options so that I wouldn't feel left out. Even better, these same people asked me how to keep the cross-contamination at bay, making me feel safe, and very, very full. I try hard to remember those kindnesses when I have people over who can't have one of my favorite foods. Cheese. That favorite food would be cheese.

Disappearing Allergies

Another part of this food allergy life that is so confusing to parents everywhere (myself included) is the whole "growing out of it" business. I've had kid guests who used to be tree-nut allergic as preschoolers and are now able to tolerate the occasional almond. My own daughter had a slight allergy to egg whites and citrus and berries and is now able to eat all of the above with no issues. There is no magic bullet to cure food allergies in kids and no way of knowing if your kid will be lucky enough to outgrow his. It can also be disconcerting to parents who previously shielded their child from a food that showed up reactive on his blood test to say, "Let him have at it!" Those "what-ifs" can make a mother crazy.

While it may be frustrating for me to embrace tangerines again, and extremely annoying for me to update my daughter's school about the changes in her diet, imagine how it must be on the school's end. Or for friends and relatives who may be feeding her for the weekend. You can see how some people who are not living with food allergies daily may get frustrated with those of us who are. I would suggest two things on the part of all parents involved: communication and patience.

Always let parents who are preparing food for your allergic (or previously allergic) child know exactly where she stands, food-wise. Be clear and non-hysterical and offer suggestions for snacks or even send allergy-safe treats with your child. Parents who are hosting, please have a little patience with those of us who are trying to keep our kids safe. We, like you, are doing the best we can, and part of that means letting our child have a normal life filled with playdates, birthday parties, sleepovers, and midnight refrigerator raids. And we promise to limit our use of ALL CAPS in any communications, whatsoever.

#siblinglife

Unless you have an only child or a house filled with kids with allergies, you're going to have another issue on your hands while trying to keep your dairy allergy kid safe and well fed. Making everyone in the house give up ice cream is going to be incredibly upsetting for 10-year-old milkshake-lovers. How those siblings react in the face of a food-allergic comrade can be wildly different. Siblings can be a blessing in this regard, or they can be a nightmare of epic proportions. I have an older brother. I know the pain of the older sibling.

WHEN YOUR FUR BABY IS SICK

Oh no, I didn't.

As a woman who lives in the world in the 21st century, I know how many people consider their dog, cat, gerbil, or horse their "baby." And that's totally fine. If you choose pets over kids, you're probably going to have loads of money left over to bail out the global economy when the rest of us destroy it by eventually rejecting kale. (It's going to happen, mark my words.) Even though vet bills aren't the same as tuition for the children, one thing that fur babies and real babies have in common is allergies.

I first noticed gluten-free dog food when I received my own celiac diagnosis. Being a human being at the top of some kind of food chain, I assumed the gluten-free dog food was for people like me who had licky dogs and could react badly if that dog slobber had gluten in it, in addition to all that love. Turns out, being humanist makes one blind.

Dogs and cats suffer from food allergies AND food intolerances. Just like us! Dogs and cats are also like humans in that baby animals may grow out of their food allergies, and their physical symptoms are the same as our allergic reactions. Signs your dog or cat may have a food allergy include red and itchy skin, obsessive chewing on paws, bleeding skin, rashes, itchy butt, and hair loss. Dog or cat food intolerances generally result in stomach upset, vomiting, and diarrhea. Sound familiar?

Your pet's veterinarian will also diagnose your dog or cat in the same manner she will diagnose your child: the dreaded elimination diet. Yep, an elimination of suspected allergens followed by a food challenge is how you find out what foods your little fluff ball of love is allergic to, or intolerant of. Interestingly enough, animals do have different common allergens than people. Probably because a dog or cat diet is much higher in lamb, pork, and corn than the average human diet.

The top allergens for dogs include beef, dairy, wheat, egg, chicken, lamb, soy, pork, rabbit, and fish. And cats' top allergens include beef, lamb, seafood, corn, soy, dairy, and gluten. Stupid gluten. And most animals will have more than one allergy, so you have that to look forward to when shopping for kibble. So get all the babies checked out, and feed them accordingly. You don't want an itchy diarrhea butt on your hands. Or at least not another one.

I've seen siblings be the best possible advocates for a sister with a disability, and I've seen siblings tease the celiac kid mercilessly about doughnuts. No matter which type of brothers and sisters reside in your own home, I have the same advice: Give the kid a break. Yes, I'm talking about the nonallergic kid, for once.

IS MY CHILD ALLERGIC OR AM I JUST CRAZY?

Because you should know.

Maybe you've been noticing a little redness around the corners of Jackson's mouth lately after he eats almond butter. Or, perhaps you just think Emma is totally sluggish every time pasta night comes around. It's supereasy to get caught up in the food allergy game when it's all parents at the park are talking about. You begin to see danger in every granola bar, and it's making you crazy. Before you start announcing that Timatha has a corn allergy, take this quiz. Then talk to a doctor because, seriously, this quiz is not a medical diagnosis.

Am I Crazy?

1. I only eat organic food when:

(a) It's important, such as in foods where antibiotics could be added (dairy, meat) and in certain vegetables that are more likely to have residual pesticides (the Dirty Dozen[3]).

(b) It's on sale.

(c) All of the time, because there are toxins in every single thing, including lip balm. If you don't choose organic everything from gummy bears to your pencils, you will get cancer and die.

2. I think gluten is:

(a) Something that everyone is talking about but is basically harmful to people with celiac disease, a gluten intolerance, a wheat allergy, or other health problems of the autoimmune system.

(b) A huge trend.

(c) Poison. Everyone who eats gluten will get cancer and die.

Every now and then, take the nonallergic kids out for a treat that won't fly in your home. Let them go crazy and only hose them down and sanitize them right before you get home so as not to rain on the gluten parade. I'm assuming you've already had the talk about not bragging to the peanut-allergic kid that you "just ate the hell out of a Reese's fountain," yes? If not, make sure you take

---

3. My kid says he's allergic to broccoli, but the allergist says he's most likely not. I think:

(a) He's full of shit.

(b) He's a genius, but still full of shit.

(c) His body is telling him something, and I trust him fully. Obviously, if he eats broccoli, he will get cancer and die.

4. I feel a little sleepy after I eat ice cream, and my kid gets superhyper. From this information, I must conclude that:

(a) Sugar makes my kid hyper, and maybe I need more sleep.

(b) Dairy and sugar treats should be a "sometimes" food.

(c) We're both allergic to dairy, and we're going to get cancer and die.

5. I don't believe what my doctor says about anything, because:

(a) She ignored me when I gave her my mother's (my child's grandmother's) medical history.

(b) She's also wearing a "Make America Great Again" hat.

(c) I know better than any doctor even though I never even considered medical school because science isn't real. And, I'm going to get cancer and die.

You know if you answered all "c," you're crazy, right? Oh no, you don't know that because most crazy people don't actually realize they are crazy. Well now you do! Please go see someone who is a mental health professional before you cut out any more deliciousness from your diet.

your other kids aside and make sure that they understand how hurtful that could be to their sibling. Then, just deal. Because no matter what the illness, kids can be assholes. If one kid tries to brag about his peanut butter–pretzel ice cream to the kid with every one of those problems, he's going to do it no matter what you say. Give the proper consequence, and then take it easy. These are kids, and they're not perfect. As long as the teasing involves words, and never, ever involves trying to hide the allergen in the allergic sibling's lunch. Annoying siblings who call each other names is just life. It's dealable.

The good news is that you'll be teaching your other kids a whole shit ton of empathy without even trying. The bad news is: resentment, resentment, and more resentment. On both sides, actually.

Medical Disclaimer

While this book will be chock-full of information, please do have a long and detailed conversation with your doctor about your child's allergy/intolerance/autoimmune disease diagnosis. Ask every single question in the world, including the very important: Do I need an EpiPen? If you need one, you're probably going to need two. Do I have to take my child to the emergency room the second I use an EpiPen? What's the worst-case scenario here? These are questions you MUST ask your doctor, because I'm here to tell you how to eat yums and live life—and I am not a medical professional. Please, please, please use this book as a lifestyle and cupcake guide, and save the rest of your questions for a real MD.

Chapter

2

You're Doing It Wrong

Hey parents, how does it feel to be in the age of mass judgment about every damn thing you do? Great? Yes, that was certainly how I felt when a dad in my son's kindergarten class spent a good 10 minutes lecturing me after *his* son now possessed the ability to use at least three curse words in a sentence, and correctly. And let me tell you how great I felt after showing up with the post–basketball game snack and not realizing I'd picked up packs of Trader Joe's trail mix that was chock-full of not just peanuts, but tree nuts as well. It was a rough time in my life, and the fact that I'd even managed to make it to my kid's basketball game was impressive. Bringing two major allergens to feed 6- and 7-year-olds? Not so impressive. So, yeah, as parents WE ARE getting judged all of the time. All. Of. The. Time. And if we were to be honest here, we'd also cop to doing some pretty harsh judging of other parents ourselves. Let me just leave this here for you: Honey Boo Boo.

While I'd like to teach the world to sing in perfect harmony, my goal with this book (and this chapter) is to shed some light on both sides of the aisle and help us understand each other a little bit better—and maybe have some empathy when that clueless mom shows up with peanut butter cookies to feed the Boy Scouts. Or when that hysterical dad inspects every single dish for gluten at the end-of-year cookout. We're all trying our best here, and I'd love it if both types of parents would garner some sympathy, instead of eye rolling. Or eye rolling coupled with sympathy, even. If being armed with the facts about food allergies and how difficult it can be to parent a child who can't eat normal cupcakes doesn't help you feel a little bit more compassion for the dairy-free family, well, perhaps you're just a great big ol' asshole. But I'm going to assume you are not. And I'd appreciate it if you would, for the time it takes to read this book, hold onto the assumption that I am also not a great big ol' asshole. What you do on your own time, after finishing the Resources section, is totally up to you.

Why Am I Even Reading This G*@# D^%! Book?

Hi there, friend. It's so nice of you to stick around so far even after I warned you away from delicious dairy. That's how I know you're committed to making the world a better place. Or at least making your child and his friends happy and healthy. The payoff is about to happen, as this is the part where I convince everyone to get along and to break (gluten-free, dairy-free, soy-free) bread together. Or at least I try. I know there are some of you out there who are only hate reading so you can see how mad I make you, and no way are you going to eat gluten-free bread just to make someone or someone else's kid happy. You are the parent I hope to reach, even though it can be hard to break through to someone who is pretty convinced that we're all faking our diarrhea. Although how one would fake diarrhea is really beyond me. Or why anyone would want to, just to one-up the members of the PTA. Still, you're suspicious, and I like that.

Here is where I'd like to address the why-should-I-give-a-damn population of parents and caretakers. I'm going to explore the arguments I've heard from parents who are sick and tired of other kids being sick and tired, the parents who are superpissed that their child's favorite PB&J is banned from the lunchroom, and the parents who cannot hear the word "gluten" even one more time before losing their ever-loving minds. Because I get it! If you make a nice lunch for a kid, and someone tells you that it's jacked up, you're going to take that as an insult. Putting aside the drudgery that is making kids' school lunches, whipping up something for the bake sale, or trying to sort out what to serve at a playdate, preparing food and having it rejected—for whatever reason—is an emotional gut punch. And you know who punches people in the gut? Bullies. Parents who are being told they are sending the wrong food to school/to Jane's house/to the bake sale are essentially being given a beat down by the school bully. That's what it feels like, and it tends to make one skittish and defensive. These feelings are valid.

Add to this element the time crunch we're under as busy, modern parents and the pickiness of our own children, and DAMN. Being concerned about everyone else's lunch sounds like a whole load of bullshit. Sometimes, it's all you can do to throw a cheese stick and a muffin into your kid's snack bag and call it a day. I've been there, and I will be there again. That does not make one a bad parent, it makes one a normal parent on a day when going the extra mile is absolutely impossible. What I want all of you overwhelmed parents to understand is that I'm not asking you to work hard every day to remove the eight main allergens from your child's very existence. No one is asking that, and if they are, they should probably be paying you a zillion dollars for the service. My goal is simply to get you to come around every now and then and make sure there's a little something for the allergic kids at your child's birthday party. Or that you choose the least allergy-laden option to prepare for a bake sale every now and then. Hell, go crazy with your chocolate cheesecake bites when you want to, just every now and then, make one for the kids who wish they could eat cheesecake that wasn't of the vegan variety. I'm not asking you to completely turn your life around with only one big exception: peanuts.

Please guys: Just stop with the peanut butter and peanut snacks in public places. It's honestly not that hard to avoid this one major allergen outside your own home. Since peanuts can be deadly even in the tiniest amounts (not for every kid, not even for most kids), it's just one thing to avoid when you're taking food anywhere that allergic kids may be gathering. While most schools do have a ban on peanut products, there are still a lot of defiant parents out there who insist that the threat is being exaggerated and eff 'em if they can't take it. Survival of the fittest and all that. Stop the madness. Really. It's one small thing you can do for the safety of the peanut-allergy kids everywhere. While the estimate is somewhere between 150 to 200 who die of food allergies each year in the United States, more than 50 percent of those deaths are from peanut allergies.[1] A heck of a lot is also due to dairy allergies, which is also terrifying, and must be noted. I personally enjoy peanut butter in my own home; I just don't bring it around kids outside of the ones I know are 100 percent safe. If you're a person who can't handle only eating peanut butter at home and away from kids, well, I'm not sure how you really function in society. Please do enlighten me when you take a break from writing your threatening letters to all of the world's leaders and trolling Internet sites for fun. Or don't, actually.

We, as a society, have gone pretty far afield at times with the bootstraps stuff. While I'm a big believer in taking care of your own damn self, I also believe in taking care of your fellow man when that fellow man is in need. Or, just when I feel like being a decent human being. Are there times when I've screwed the pooch? You bet. See the trail mix example above, and every time I brought my favorite batch of gluten-free Monster cookies to an event where I didn't even stop to think that there might be kids there I know nothing about, who could therefore be deathly allergic to peanuts. I'm not asking everyone to be perfect, because God knows that none of us can achieve that in a day that also requires us to carpool. I'm just asking for your consideration. And for all of you food allergy deniers to understand that we're not fucking around here; this is serious business. We all love our kids, and we all know how horrific it would be for harm to come to our children. Before you defiantly pack peanut butter for your child's lunch or traveling basketball team snack, please, please, please consider an alternative.

I'm Trying, But People Are Such Effers!

Yes, it's true. No matter how hard you try to make food safe for people with food issues, someone could still complain. I like to call them vegans. I kid, but yes, it's really hard to feel good about being a team player when someone on the team is going to call out that one dish that may have fish sauce . . . but you didn't know it was fish sauce because it was called something else, and you don't read Korean. It really makes one not want to try at all, and I get it, because I have totally been there on more than one occasion. I have a gluten-free blog, as you may or may not know, but I get constant complaints that something has dairy in it, or someone is allergic to corn, or someone is tired of all of my cursing. Whatever. I cannot please 100 percent of the people 100 percent of the time, and I'm not asking you to do that, either. I can ignore people who complain after I've made a big effort, or I can listen carefully and ponder what I could change the next time I'm feeding a big group of people. I'll be honest: I do both. Sometimes, it's worth it to consider expanding your meal to include other food restrictions. It's also very satisfying to feed people safely in your own home. Other times, it's such a pain in the ass that you just have to take everyone to the salad bar at Whole Foods and tell them to fend for themselves. All of this is okay. Do the best that you can, and be honest. If someone is going to be a jerk to you after all of that, never, ever, ever invite him to your home ever again. Move on, and don't look back. Also, YOU ARE AWESOME, AND PLEASE INVITE ME OVER.

When we're talking about kids, however, remember that they may not yet be capable of preparing their own safe meals. Special consideration must be made in the case of those little people, but it's not that hard! Really!

Here's a simple guide to preparing food for kids.

Every Day: Follow school guidelines on allergens.

Special Occasions: Try to make as many kids happy as possible without losing your shit. In lieu of making every kid happy, communicate with allergic kids' parents so that they can take on the job of making their kids happy.

There. That's it!

I'm attempting to appeal to your humanity here, so again, if you're just a big ol' A, please move on and maybe relocate to the Galapagos,[2] where apparently there are no food allergies.

But None of Our Grandparents Had Food Allergies!

It's impossible to truly measure the history of food allergies, since modern medicine is obviously so much more advanced than it was in the time of our ancestors. Anecdotally, I can tell you that I had a great-grandmother who had constant stomach ailments and did eventually die of stomach cancer. Was she ever tested for celiac? Nope. But along with the other autoimmune diseases my family battles today, I have celiac, and it's heredity. It's highly likely that my great-grandmother went untreated for celiac disease and eventually succumbed to the effects. It's just that no one around her knew about celiac at the time, and medicine during that time, and all of time before, was not equipped to deal with her issues. I mean, has anyone ever seen *Downton Abbey*? Really.

Another family anecdote I'll share, because I know you guys are dying to know all about my family history, illustrates the way food allergies were handled in the past versus how we talk about food allergies in the present. My grandfather had a severe strawberry allergy his entire life, and I never knew this until a few years ago when discussing my own daughter's reaction to strawberries and citrus with my Aunt Shirley. Shirley informed me that my daughter came by it honestly, as her father (my grandfather) was deathly allergic to strawberries. Also, wow, thanks for scaring the crap out of me, Shirl. While my daughter seems to have outgrown her allergy, my grandfather did not. And while her entire school, social group, and extended family knew all about her skin reaction when her little lips touched specific fruits, no one but my grandfather's immediate family knew, or cared, about his strawberry thing. Why? Probably because my grandfather lived in a time where you only ate at home. Thus eliminating the need for an all-points bulletin and demand to scrub the school cafeteria of strawberry essence. He ate at home and brought his lunch to school and then, later, to work. The few times he ever did dine out, he simply did not order strawberries.

I could not tell you the last time my kids ate every meal at home for an entire week, or even a long weekend. We're much more mobile today, and our kids are, too. I'm also guessing that during my grandfather's day, there wasn't an obnoxious kid starting food fights or some asshole smearing peanut butter on the allergic kid's desk. It was a different time. A more polite time, when people did all of their hating behind closed doors.

My point is, the argument of "no one used to have food allergies" is bullshit. People did, people died, and people also didn't blog about it or get into arguments about the validity of it on Facebook. So let's just put that to rest and agree that comparing our children today to the children of the 1890s is unrealistic, and not just because of the whole "scabies is just a part of urban life" thing.

Intolerant to Intolerance

In the past, before the great food wars of the 2000s, a person might say a certain food doesn't agree with her while explaining why she's skipping dessert and coffee. Today, we have a much more official-sounding term: *intolerant*. If you live and dine in North America, you've heard people complain about being lactose intolerant, gluten intolerant, and annoying person intolerant many times before. I'll admit to using that last one to get a different airplane seat assignment more than once. I blame the term *intolerant* for so much of the confusion and irritation over food allergies and conditions. It can be frustrating to those who eat freely to understand what someone means when he says that he is a very specific (and usually delicious) type of food intolerant. It usually inspires one of two reactions: panic or eye rolling.

Food allergies and food intolerances are actually very different beings, with the former being much more dangerous and needing to be taken more seriously. To get an official definition, I talked with registered dietician at the UCLA Digestive Health and Nutrition Clinic Nancee Jaffe. Jaffe explains the differences between allergies and intolerances like so: "Intolerances are, by definition, not harmful to the body as there is no immune reaction, just uncomfortable and bothersome symptoms." Adding confusion to the issues, Jaffe explains that food intolerances are also on the rise. Jaffe reports that "according to FARE (Food Allergy Research and Education), food allergies increased in children by somewhere between 18 to 50 percent in the years 1997 through 2011. There are lots of theories, but I don't think there is a definite reason for the rise. I would assume it is a combination of changes to environment, food processing, food-consumption patterns, gut microbiome, genetics, and stress reactions in the body/inflammation." So it's a thing, you guys. An uncomfortable, gassy thing.

Allergies are much more hard-core than food intolerances and do need to be taken more seriously, with symptoms ranging from itchiness to death. So, while you need to be uncompromising in your attention to detail when preparing food for an allergic kid, intolerances are not going to have the same short- or long-term effect.

For those of you who have a food intolerance, please do not think I am minimizing your pain. I've had people describe the symptoms associated with their gluten intolerance, and I wouldn't wish that on my worst enemy. Throwing up blood, anyone? You can get knocked out of school, work, special events, and more if you are slipped a food that your body does not tolerate. It's serious business; it's just not life-threatening. Of course, not every food issue needs to be life-threatening to be taken seriously. And, in a perfect world, everyone would be able to eat safely and happily no matter what issues, intolerances, autoimmune diseases, and allergies existed. But we do not live in a perfect world, and we need to figure out how to all get along without anyone getting hurt. No, getting butt hurt does not count.

So, if you're someone who has a food intolerance, you will have to work harder to get some people to take you seriously. It simply comes with the territory. And if you're someone who is trying to keep your 8-year-old's soccer team safe, remember that an allergy is deadly serious. Plus, as Jaffee adds, "Patients often assume that they have a sensitivity or intolerance if they had one bad incident with a particular food, such as a bout of diarrhea or a little bit of excess gas production." So, yeah, *intolerance* is a term thrown around to describe anything that might be irritating.

BUT.

You knew there was more but talk, didn't you? If your child seems to have a food intolerance, do not simply rely on the kindness of strangers to keep your child from swelling up or throwing up. Go see your pediatrician, allergist, gastroenterologist, and every single doctor you can see to make sure that, without a doubt, it is an intolerance and not an allergy, which could have much more serious long-term consequences. It's not enough to decide that your child has a food intolerance: For his safety, you MUST see a qualified physician. And if that physician doesn't give you an answer, keep going until you get one. It really can help your kiddos while easing the resentment of the nonallergic by having a very clear answer when someone asks, "Does your child have any food issues?" The more information parents have and share in a noncondescending manner, the easier it will be to find common ground at the dining room table, which is currently covered in *Star Wars* decor because every single kid from now until this portion of the series ends WILL be having a *Star Wars* party. This we can all agree upon.

Also, please don't describe a like or a dislike as an intolerance. It's so not cool to panic the people making your food because you think cilantro tastes like soap. On that note, aren't there enough people in the world who think cilantro tastes like soap to discourage everyone from using it? No? Not yet? Okay, we'll wait.

The last word on food intolerances for those who think that they are bullshit: Being intolerant of a certain food is not, actually, bullshit. If you're around my husband after he eats ice cream, you'll see (and hear) a very clear example of a reaction that is not allergic in nature, but very, very not good. While you won't kill anyone who is lactose intolerant with a drop of cream in her cocoa, you will make her uncomfortable. It's up to you to decide whether you want your guests to be comfortable or uncomfortable after dining at your child's pool party. And by that I mean uncomfortable in a dietary sense, because we're all pretty uncomfortable with pool parties. Can we just admit that already and cover up and not worry about our child drowning and ruining Maeve's birthday? Okay, thanks.

Chapter

3

So Is My Kid Just Supposed to Eat Air?

Holy jeez, you got ANOTHER email about a fish-stick allergy at your 3rd grader's lunch table. Or maybe you keep falling asleep reading the instructions about in-class party treat regulations. The point is, shit is going down, and that shit is in the food you're sending to school with your precious little (gluten-free, dairy-free, soy-free) muffin. It's time to evaluate your lunch boxes, people, whether it's your muffin that needs to be gluten- and dairy-free or the muffin sharing a lunch table with your kiddo.

Whether you've been dairy-free since before it was cool, or you simply cannot wrap your head around how soy gets into every damn thing, the whole food issues spectrum can be super-duper confusing. Those of us who can't hang with gluten know everything about it and what horrible things can happen to our bodies if we accidentally get a smidge in our chocolate cake holes. But that does not make us experts on, say, lactose. People dealing with nut allergies may shake their heads in confusion at the egg allergic. What this means is that every dang one of us has a lot to learn about food allergies and diseases that are food related. No one is an expert on every food danger out there, but you're about to get an overview of the most common forbidden foods you'll hear about on the playground. In addition to the eight main allergens, I'm going to throw in a few more items since other diseases can be exacerbated by certain foods. Let's learn about all of these foods that can jack your playdate together, shall we?

Please note: If you or your child have had a reaction to any of these foods, or have been diagnosed with any food allergies AT ALL, talk to your doctor and an allergist about keeping yourself and your offspring safe. This is informational, not a prescription. I keep saying this over and over because no matter how many episodes of *Grey's Anatomy* I may have watched, I am still not a doctor.

Gluten

The OG devil that got me into the food issue game, gluten is the protein found in wheat, barley, rye, and triticale (the hybrid grain of wheat and rye). As a celiac, gluten is what tears up my gut and causes long-term negative health effects. But when you're talking about allergies, a wheat allergy is more likely the culprit than a gluten allergy, which is all-encompassing. But if you cut out all gluten, you will cut out wheat, so the wheat allergic are essentially gluten-free.

Most people think gluten equals bread and pasta, but that's only part of the story. Gluten, like many other allergens, can be found in sneaky places in the form of flavorings and thickeners. Barley malt is a culprit in everything from candy to beer. Though your kids are probably not drinking beer, right? Right??? And soy sauce is often made with fermented wheat. Some sushi rice is made with wheat vinegar, and some crazy people put flour in queso. One of the biggest gluten dangers comes when you're enjoying anything at all fried, even if it has no flour coating. Gluten is a very sticky protein, and if your food comes into contact with it via a shared platter, fryer, or bowl, it can stick onto your "safe" food and make you sick. This means that French fries must be thoroughly vetted before being deemed safe for your gluten-free consumption. While I may be incredibly well informed about the hidden sources of gluten, the "hidden" factor is an issue that you'll find with so many of these other allergens when you venture outside of your own kitchen. My advice to everyone with gluten, soy, egg, or any of the other problems is to always ask about ingredients and preparation before eating anything that is not a whole food or any food that you did not prepare yourself.

Where to look for gluten: bread, pastries, sauces, dressings, fried foods, soy sauce, seitan and other meat substitutes, cereals, beer, oatmeal, processed foods and drinks, and candy.

Dairy

Dairy refers to milk from animals such as cows, sheep, goats, and camels (not common in North America, but elsewhere) or products made from animal milk. Yes, this means cheese, dammit. A dairy allergy is a reaction to the protein found in milk and milk products, and it can be as severe as the dreaded peanut allergy, depending on the allergic individual. Casein is the protein in milk, along with whey, that people should also look out for when reading labels. Some hot dogs, sausages, and lunchmeats contain casein, even though it is not a main ingredient, so you have to read labels very carefully. Dairy is also one of those ingredients that can sneak into so many things in the forms of butter, casein, whey, or something as far removed as breadcrumbs on top of your dairy-free mac and cheese. Like gluten, dairy is such a staple of the American diet that we don't even think about certain foods, usually carbohydrates, containing dairy. Any baked good has a strong possibility of having dairy as an ingredient in the form of butter or milk. Again, this is why you have to ask about every single ingredient when you're not dining at home or overseeing your meal, and stress that you have an allergy when speaking with whoever is serving up your dinner.

A dairy allergy is not the same thing as lactose intolerance, and is, in fact, much more severe. Hence the reminder to stress the allergy parts of the conversation, as many people are lactose intolerant but do not face the same risks as those with allergies.

Lactose intolerance exists when you are lacking enough of the enzyme lactase to break down the sugar in lactose, which is found in milk and dairy products. Typical reactions to lactose include gas, bloating, diarrhea, nausea, and stomach pain, and lactose intolerance can develop at any age. In fact, lactose intolerance does become more common as we age, meaning the older population has a much greater incidence of lactose intolerance than any other group.

While uncomfortable, lactose intolerance is not life-threatening, and depending on your level of intolerance, you can pop a Lactaid before going into dairy territory, although avoidance is certainly the safer choice. Alas, the allergic do not have a pill that can put their reactions on hold if they accidentally ingest dairy. The first line of defense is offense when dealing with an allergy, which means ask, ask, ask, and bring your own food when you're not sure if a dairy-free option will be made available. Luckily, with the popularity of veganism taking off, you'll know you can eat safely at a vegan restaurant or with a crowd of vegans. Especially important is that your dairy-free dish won't be in danger of getting mixed up or cooked in the same pot as one with dairy when you're dining vegan-style. Still, you must communicate often, and clearly, to anyone who is preparing food for you. Dairy is one of the most complicated because of its ubiquitousness in our society and also because it is the most common food allergen. It's so sad that it's also the most delicious.

A note about milk from animals other than cows. While there are a certain percentage of people who have a dairy allergy that can tolerate goat or sheep milk, not everyone can. Depending on the severity of your reaction, you can try to experiment with other types of milks, knowing that goat's and sheep's milk is still dairy. Additionally, a blood test can be helpful in figuring out if alternative milk is an answer. For the lactose intolerant, however, lactose is lactose no matter what animal's milk is being consumed.

Watch for: milk, cheese, butter, ice cream, breads, baked desserts, whey, pudding/mousse, yogurt, nougat, *kefir*, soups, cream sauces, *ghee*, casein, some pastas (not all), some lunchmeats (not all).

Peanuts

Eff peanuts, man. While I may enjoy a piece of gluten-free matzo with a schmear of peanut butter, I still rue the day that peanut butter was ever marketed to children. Of course, I should really be ruing the day that peanut allergies suddenly spiked, and thus started scaring the crap out of parents everywhere. While no one can exactly pinpoint when the rise in nut allergies began, between 1997 and 2008, the incidence of peanut and tree-nut allergies nearly tripled.[1] Given the severity of reactions in nut allergies, a lot of research has been, and continues to be, done to find answers to the increase and how to prevent deadly reactions among the allergic.

Most recently, the *New England Journal of Medicine* published a study[2] wherein babies who were at a high risk of developing a peanut allergy were fed a peanut butter mush once solid foods were introduced (around 4 months or later). The study found that these infants were 80 percent less likely to develop a peanut allergy. While this certainly would give a new parent some hope in avoiding an allergic kiddo, please do discuss this with your doctor to see what's best for your family before slinging the mush around your house.

Of course, most of you are reading this because you already have or know an allergic kid, so that ship has sailed. At this juncture, it's about strict avoidance of peanuts or peanut products, or any processed food with peanuts or peanut butter ingredients. I stress strict avoidance in the case of peanut allergies, because even the smallest trace of peanuts can cause a severe allergic reaction in the severely allergic. I had a meeting with a man who was explaining his nephew's severe peanut allergy. As a man who indulged in PB, he admitted that he might have spilled some on his shirt that day. He also knew that he would have to stay away from his nephew on that particular day, given the fact that little kids are probably grabbing height of his peanut-buttery shirt.

While it's not actually true that peanuts "in the air" can cause an allergic reaction, any amount ingested at all certainly can. This may seem extreme, but in the case of deadly allergies, no risk is worth the possible outcome. Which is why a ban on peanut products in the classroom where an allergic kid is makes so much sense. Kids are messy, and they smear their food all around the place. If the danger is so high that it's a matter of life or death, don't let anyone smear that brown death around any kids. Once a child is an adult and is more able to control his own environment, he probably won't be sitting so close to his lunch mates that he could find his left elbow in Tupperware full of peanut butter. But when kids are still in school, brains not fully developed, and trapped in the same spaces for mealtime, we owe it to them to make it as safe as possible.

I'm guessing that you, like me, have seen the resistance some parents can have to a peanut or nut ban at school. It seems to be one of those hot topics, even though I cannot understand how it compares to, say, vaccines. (Oh no, I'm not stepping on that minefield today. We can discuss that in person, and not in front of Jenny McCarthy.) I'm also guessing that you've been in similar meetings like I have where someone brought up the no-peanuts rule, and a mom declared, "That's all my kid will eat!" What is one to do? Of course, we've all dealt with picky eaters in our homes, and if you haven't, please shut up now. Thanks. So what's a parent to do when her child demands peanut butter sandwiches for every meal?

First of all, that seems problematic, nutrition-wise. Still, having two demanding children of my own, I can kind of relate. On more than one occasion, my kids have begged for peanut butter crackers in their lunches. I know that they're good and crunchy and all that, so I see the attraction. That attraction that makes their tiny voices go up several notches when they screech, "But I swear, no one I sit next to has an allergy!" Or, "Ple-e-e-e-ase! It's the ONLY thing I want!" It's relentless, the begging for food thing. And annoying. And it can wear down any parent who is feeling vulnerable. I do believe I have a solution to the constant demands for peanut butter in public places, and I'm going to share it with you. When my kids ask me for peanut butter in their lunch boxes for the one-thousandth time, here's what I do: I say, "No."

Wow, I did not mean to go off on a peanut tangent, but there it is. Seriously, SunButter instead is NOT SO BAD, people.

Watch for: peanuts, peanut butter, candy bars, cookies, protein bars, trail mix, Cracker Jacks, and other popcorn treats.

Tree Nuts

Just a little FYI about tree nuts, and why they are a separate species than the peanut. Peanuts are actually legumes (I know! It's crazy). And tree nuts are nuts that, well, grow on trees. Peanuts come up out of the ground like their legume friends, the green bean, the green pea, soybeans, and many more. So now you know!

One reason that tree-nut allergies are so complicated is that they can include just a few tree nuts like almonds, walnuts, and pistachios, or they can expand to sesame seeds, which are not technically tree nuts but do have similar properties and are cross-reactive to some kids with tree-nut allergies—and its products (oh no, hummus!!!!) and beyond to coconut (which is rare). Whether you have the kid with the allergy, or you know one, be sure that everyone is 100 percent clear about which nuts are the dangerous ones. Many, many times, those of us who try to cook allergy-free reach for the coconut oil, and we need to know if that's not going to be okay for our littlest diners. Another thing you need to consider if your child has a tree-nut allergy is the cross-contamination that can take place in processing foods. Read every label before feeding your allergic kids, because some foods can be processed on shared equipment with tree nuts.

With peanut allergies getting all of the headlines, the tree-nut kids can be not taken as seriously, or just confused with the peanut kids and given a spoonful of almond butter at a playdate. It makes it all the more important for parents to communicate thoroughly and frequently with anyone who might be preparing food for their children. It's also crucial to teach the little tree-nutters extensively about their allergies, so the kiddos can fend for themselves out in the real world, where trail mix is omnipresent. This goes for every kid with an allergy, of course. I simply reiterate it here because tree-nut allergies can be dismissed, but as we've covered before, any food allergy can be deadly, and they all must be taken seriously.

Where you find tree nuts: walnuts, almonds, pecans, macadamia nuts, hazelnuts, cashews, chestnuts, pistachios, Brazil nuts, pine nuts, marzipan, pesto, pralines, nut butters, nut flours, nut oils, nut milks, Nutella, and, of course, candy bars.

Watch for: sesame seeds, tahini, hummus, halva, and buns with sesame seeds.

Sugar

One of the fastest-rising food issues is sugar, which is not an allergy but can be just as damaging, and it is dang near impossible to avoid in childhood circles. While I personally don't avoid most sugars when I'm cooking for the kiddos, I will certainly make the exception for kids who require a low- or no-sugar diet. Parents, please be aware that celiac and diabetes often go hand-in-hand, so check on that when you have a gluten-free partygoer coming over.

Most kids who are diabetic are very familiar with what is okay to eat and what is not okay to eat. The kids I've met are expert blood sugar testers and the first to step up and say, "No, thank you" to an offending treat. I made the mistake at my son's birthday party of asking a diabetic guest's father if he could have some of the gummy snacks I'd laid out. The little guy didn't roll his eyes at me when his father smiled and said yes, but I felt like he could have, and it would have been well deserved. Still, please have the sugar conversation with a parent of a child who is hypoglycemic or diabetic. It's a dangerous disease, if not monitored carefully. I'll cover sugar more extensively in Chapter 4, so consider this just a heads-up!

Watch for: everything good.

Soy

The first time I heard of someone with a soy allergy, I thought, "Well, that must be easy to avoid." After all, soybeans and soy products are usually found in Asian cuisine. You have your edamame, your soy sauce, your tofu, and your miso. Just don't order Chinese takeout or sushi! Well, that's not exactly accurate, even though soy is found in larger quantities in many Asian cuisines: Chinese, Japanese, Korean, Thai, Mongolian, and more.

You never realize how much soy is added into processed foods until you find yourself, or someone you hang out with, allergic to soy. The good news is, however, that most children with soy allergies outgrow them. But, until those little ones are free and clear, you have to become an expert at reading labels and home-cooking to keep them safe. Soy is an additive that can be found in ice cream, in packaged baked goods, and in so many protein bars. It's basically the most popular additive on the block. And with the rise of veganism, soy was one of the first dairy alternatives that seemed to create a better quality of cheese and milk products without using animal milks. I still prefer soy milk to normal when I get my latte at Starbucks. Possibly because I'm used to having soy around. We all are! We just don't realize that it's so flipping prevalent. Also, if you're trying to keep genetically modified organisms (GMOs) out of your life, most soy is genetically modified. So there's that. So keep your eyes peeled and read the label of any food that comes in a package. Ask the soy question about every dish your allergic kid wants to eat at a restaurant. Keep on it, because soy is sneaky.

Watch for: tofu, soy sauce, wheat-free tamari, tempeh, miso, edamame, soybean oil, soy milk, candy bars, flavorings, gluten-free processed foods, gluten-free flour blends, fried foods, vegan cheeses, vegan processed foods, and protein bars.

Eggs

Egg allergies may be rare, but they've been around for a very long time. In fact, I believe most of us probably heard of egg allergies long before allergies to soy, gluten, or tree nuts. While you may think that it's no biggie to skip the sunny-side-up breakfast, eggs appear in many more delicious forms that the allergic need to be aware of when they sit down to every meal. You know what I'm talking about: dessert.

A fluffy cake is fluffy, at least in part, because of eggs. A meringue is eggs and sugar, and it equals awesomeness. Eggs are a crucial ingredient in so many desserts that you may wonder how in the world the egg allergic ever enjoy the best part of a meal. (Hint: Check out the recipes starting on page 99.) Pasta is often made with eggs, as are most bread products. Some bagels and most pretzels are even coated in egg wash, so make sure that you're getting those vegan bagels, if you indulge. Read every single label, and also be on the lookout for meringue powder as a thickener in processed foods. When you're dining out, as always, ask your server if any sauces are being thickened with egg white before you sit down to dine. Ask if there are any breadcrumbs that may contain egg in your dish, or any specialty cocktail that has a little bit of foam that comes from egg whites. (Cocktails for you, not for your little one. Did I really have to say that?) Meatballs often have eggs as a binding agent, as do other dishes in need of a little sticking power. And don't forget the mayo, or actually, do forget the mayonnaise (unless it's vegan) because there are eggs in that dressing that finds its way into every church casserole.

Another time to be vocal about your egg allergy is in the doctor's office. Some flu shots contain a bit of egg protein, so you need to talk to your doctor before sticking your arm out for a stick. While most people won't have a reaction to the flu shot, if your allergy is severe, seek out an alternative without the presence of the allergen.

The rub with an egg allergy is that if you're allergic to chicken eggs, you're most likely allergic to all bird eggs. So, you can't try to substitute duck eggs in that soufflé, which is a bummer.

Watch for: eggs, egg whites, egg powder, meringue, baked goods, marzipan, breads and pastries, pasta, mayonnaise, meatballs, and meatloaf.

Fish

Fish is a tough one since we like to encourage our children to eat fish as part of a healthy diet, but luckily not as tough to avoid in the general kid population. There are tens of thousands of fish in the sea (just ask your grandmother), and your child may not be allergic to every type, so if it's important to you to include fish in your family's diet, talk to your doctor about safely testing to see what your child can tolerate. Usually salmon, tuna, and halibut are the most reactive fish when one is allergic, but this is certainly not every fish out there. Since cod is often used for fish and chips, perhaps your little fish-lover can still look forward to enjoying that on occasion. Find out!

Most of the time, when fish is present, it's pretty clear. But you should still read labels on any processed foods to make sure you know what your allergic child is eating. This is especially true if you're eating any prepackaged Asian foods that may use fish sauce or enjoying a Caesar salad or antipasto plate that could include anchovies. Additionally, if you're dining with someone who has a severe fish allergy, skip the seafood joint or the Asian restaurants. There is a much larger quantity of fish and fish products in the kitchen, and the cross-contact with the "safe" dish is just too great to ignore.

Watch for: salmon, tuna, bass, catfish, anchovies, halibut, cod, tilapia, trout, swordfish, mahi mahi, fish sticks, fish sauce, fish stock, Caesar salad dressing, some omega-3 vitamins.

Shellfish

Say goodbye to Lobster Thermidor Thursday, people! I know that's first and foremost on your kindergartener's mind, so I'm just putting it right out there. Shellfish allergies do seem to mean that you can't have the fanciest of foods at the buffet, but the good news is that if you have a fish allergy, you will not necessarily have a shellfish allergy, as these are two different beasts of the sea. Shellfish includes crustaceans (shrimp, lobster, and crab) as well as mollusks (oysters, scallops, and clams). Once you receive your shellfish diagnosis, you probably will want to avoid fish, but know that you do not have to, if the regular fish is prepared safely, and not in the same place as the shellfish.

I've seen more than one shellfish allergic reaction, and I tell you, I don't need to ever see that again, ever. It can be pretty severe, even if it's not deadly, and oftentimes, shellfish allergies are the most severe. I know that my husband wished he were dead one night after indulging in the forbidden crustacean. It was not okay, and I told him he was no longer allowed to do that, as only one of us should be in desperate need of the bathroom at a time.

Luckily, most kids are not clamoring for shellfish, and it can be relatively easy to decrease exposure for your allergic kiddo. Again, read the labels to avoid sneaky additives, and make sure you know how to identify shellfish.

Watch for: lobster, crab, shrimp, scallops, oysters, clams, mussels, squid, octopus, sea urchin, cuttlefish, snails, crawfish, fish stock, sauces, soups, and broth.

Weird Places to Find Allergens

If you happen to be dealing with a severe allergen, or just a finger-sucking baby (this is very common, as all baby mammas and daddies know), there are a few other places you need to monitor for your kiddo's allergen. For one annoying example, I just lathered up my hands with medium-expensive lotion to make sure I stay soft and supple and then realized it contained macadamia oil. Fine for me, but if I had a tree-nut allergy, or one of my kids did, it would not be my first choice at the drugstore.

While it is accurate that food allergens must be ingested into the digestive system in order for a reaction to occur, if you're really being careful, you want to avoid the allergen being in your home at all. I once scoffed at needing gluten-free makeup until I realized how many times I wiped lipstick off my teeth. A debutante, I am not. And while I'd love to pretend that I never sit around licking icing off of my fingers, my family and I know the truth. I should not be using hand lotion with gluten in it either. I'm an adult trying to sort through this mess; imagine how a 4-year-old might navigate the same.

So please be aware of any allergens in your or your child's toothpaste, lotions, makeup (yours, hopefully not your child's), oils, soaps, pet foods and snacks (I say this as a kid who once asked for Milk-Bone Dog Biscuits for Christmas. Don't judge until you've felt the clean snap of a Milk-Bone between your teeth. Fine, judge. My entire family does, so why not you?), and anything else that comes into contact with your hands, your child's hands, your child's mouth, or any other food in your home.

Labels Are HARD

I know it's a huge pain in the ass reading food labels, especially now that I'm older and require reading glasses. The more ingredients in that protein bar, the more confusing words you're going to have to look up on your phone so you know whether you're eating poison or not. Good times. But it is crucial to always read a label and make sure that what you're feeding the allergic is truly free of the offending allergen. Luckily, you can trust the "Certified Gluten Free" label with the big "GF" in the circle in the middle if you're looking for gluten-free foods, but not every allergen has its own organization working with brands to check and double-check for safety. So you get to do it!

Even if you're reading all the labels, you should be clear what is and what is not required by the Food and Drug Administration. In 1999, a study confirmed that 25 percent[3] of foods in the marketplace were not accurately displaying a label when allergens were present. Foods such as baked goods, ice cream, and candy were mislabeled, or not labeled at all, and you know those are foods that kids eat by the dozen.

In response to this information, a dedicated and vocal group of food allergy advocates worked tirelessly to address these oversights. In 2004, the Food Allergen Labeling and Consumer Protection Act (FALCPA) was passed in the United States to improve the labeling on foods. According to the FDA, "FALCPA is an amendment to the Federal Food, Drug, and Cosmetic Act and requires that the label of a food that contains an ingredient that is or contains protein from a 'major food allergen' declare the presence of the allergen in the manner described by the law."

Sometimes, you will see the allergen in the ingredient list, which is required, and also listed as "Contains: wheat" on the label. What is not required, however, is what is of concern to people who have severe reactions to allergens. Ingredients are only part of the story when you have a food allergy. The other allergens in the room are also a problem if even the slightest bit of the allergen can cause anaphylaxis or an autoimmune response. You will see many products that state, "Manufactured in a facility that also processes tree nuts" or the like, and that's when the severely allergic have to take note. But, it is not required by law for this information to be printed on the label. Which is why you have to always check changing ingredients and changing processes on any packaged foods you consume. It's enough to make you never want to eat processed food again. Which isn't the most horrible idea in the world, especially if you have a personal chef.

Additionally, there are some words that you may read on processed foods that you may not automatically know are allergens. Here are a few of the confusing words you may come across, translated into the allergen you should be looking for.

albumin = egg	nutmeat = peanuts
arachis = peanuts	ovalbumin = egg
casein = dairy	pralines = tree nuts
curds = dairy	rennet = dairy
einkorn = gluten	semolina = gluten
farina = gluten	soya = soy
globulin = egg	soy lecithin = soy
malt = gluten	whey = dairy
marzipan = tree nuts	yuba = soy

It's not easy, but you constantly have to be on your toes when you're feeding the allergic. Arming yourself with the right information will dramatically decrease the likelihood of an accidental dosing of the offending food.

What's Missing?

When I was diagnosed with celiac disease, my first stop was to see a nutritionist who could explain to me all of the vitamins and nutrients I was now going to be low on as I had to cut gluten out of my diet. It was a lot, you guys. More than I had imagined. While I need to take supplements of calcium and a multivitamin, your child's food allergy will have different nutritional repercussions. I spoke with Aaron Flores, an RDN in Los Angeles, about what he sees in his practice in relation to food intolerances and allergies among his pediatric clients. Flores works with children on all kinds of food and nutrition issues, and his advice can be similar for the allergic and nonallergic. "Obviously, my concern with any allergy is to make sure that clients can get the education they need to safely make food choices," Flores explained. "With intolerances, it is the same, but I also encourage them to really tune in to how foods are making them feel."

For all of us with food allergies, intolerance, or other disease, Flores recommends that we monitor our health, or our children's health, and listen to our bodies. Since gluten and dairy are not only common but also a dramatic removal from the diet, Flores focuses on nutrition for that specific group. "I really just educate them on proper sources of needed nutrients that can be from other foods. It's a case-by-case basis and depends on what is really going on with the kids."

Not only do you need to meet with a nutritionist to be aware of what vitamins could slip through the cracks along with all that dairy that's leaving your child's diet, you'll want to have regular checkups to make sure that your child isn't deficient in any necessary vitamins. Every child is different, and no two dairy-allergy kids will be supplementing in the same way. It's important to stay on top of what's going on in your kid's lunch box.

The Other B-Word

So now you're all clear on the contents of the lunch box, but food won't be the only challenge your allergic kid may face out in the world. Bullies prey on the weak, the different kids—or at least someone who seems to be weak or different—and having a special diet can certainly appear as a weakness, no matter how well we've trained our kids to not see it in that way. One of the great things about living in a more enlightened time is that everyone knows that bullying isn't something kids have to sit back and take. We're all aware that bullying is wrong, and bullies are getting shamed across America. And even though we can't stop Olivia from posting "nerd" on every one of Eliza's Facebook photos, we can delete and report and assume an action will be taken. Of course, when your kid has a food allergy or disorder, "action will be taken" can be too little, too late.

Even though things can sometimes go your way when your child announces his allergy (half of my daughter's class decided they were gluten-free when she received a false positive on her blood test for celiac), a lot of times that really is not the case, as in these totally weird stories, for example.

A 5-year-old in Kentucky[4] has to sit by herself at lunch because she has celiac, even though the mother keeps telling the school it's not a life-or-death situation and if she's packed her a safe lunch, she can sit anywhere. That sucks.

And is confusing because it's kind of like "keeping the kid safe" bullying, but with good intentions. Maybe?

Or how about the story of Jeremy Francoeur in Massachusetts who had egg, peanut, and shellfish allergies?[5] In addition to playing "allergy tag," wherein the kids would pretend to be something that could "kill" Jeremy, sometimes kids would lick his sandwich or throw it away, leaving him hungry at lunchtime since he could not eat the food in the school cafeteria. Naturally, Jeremy wasn't so fond of school after that. Which causes a host of other problems.

I don't share these stories to stoke your outrage, but to continue the conversation about creating safe environments for our children in every way. While we all wish bullying were something that never, ever happened, it's a reality of our time. Heck, those of us who have ever worked in an office know that there's always one bully (if not more) out to make everyone else feel insecure and, therefore, inferior to that jackass. Bullies grow up and become adult bullies (or maybe they see the error of their ways, maybe), and we all have to deal with them. So the sooner we teach our kids how to protect themselves physically and emotionally, the better.

One of the best ways to help combat bullying negatively affecting your child is to foster an open communication with your child that is supportive and not reactive. Your child is much more likely to tell you if something happened to her on the playground if you don't freak out about it as soon as she says, "pushed me down the slide." I know this is difficult, but it's crucial to develop these skills, since allergic kids can so often be targets. Dinnertime is a fabulous time to bring up food issues—aren't we all supposed to be having nonstop dinners as a family so our kids can get into Harvard? That's a thing, right? SAT scores aside, talking about how people eat different foods, and why, is a great discussion whether your family is restricted, or knows someone who has a food allergy.

Katie Hurley, LCSW, psychotherapist, and author of *The Happy Kid Handbook,* filled me in on the reality of bullying and kids with food allergies, and I have to say, I was unpleasantly surprised. Hurley told me that "1 in 13 kids in the US has food allergies (roughly 2 in every classroom), and of those kids, nearly one-third experience bullying related to their food allergies." But the crap news doesn't end there. Hurley continued, "This puts kids with food allergies at an increased risk of anxiety, depression, and/or school refusal (which leads to poor grades and the potential to drop out down the line). Bullying related to food allergies is particularly dangerous because it can put the life of the child with food allergies at risk. Sneaking ground-up walnuts into a cookie and convincing a tree-nut-allergy sufferer to eat it, for example, can result in death. Yep, the thing we're all terrified about happening, much less at the hands of another 12-year-old.

I know this makes me feel helpless, and I'm not facing the challenges a mom to a severely allergic child is facing right now. But we are not helpless, and our kids are not, either. The old-school ignore-the-bully-and-he'll-go-away advice is not accurate, Hurley explained to me. In addition to making sure that your child's school is fully informed about your child's food allergy, and the necessary actions are being taken to help keep her safe, Hurley advises the following when your food-allergic kid is dealing with challenging peers.

1. It's essential to teach kids with food allergies that it's never safe to accept food that has unknown ingredients. Never. Even if it comes from someone claiming to be a friend.

2. It's also important to teach kids to stand up tall and say "No! Stop!" and "Leave me alone!" with confidence. Role-play this at home. Talk about circumstances that can happen at school, at parties, and even during team sports, so that your child is prepared.

3. Kids with food allergies should stick with a trusted group of friends (or at least one "safe" buddy) during high-risk situations such as the lunchroom, snack time, and recess.

This advice from Hurley needs to be reinforced with your kiddos, but while remaining calm and not freaking out your child by being overly emotional. I know, it's hard. But we can't always be there. As parents, we have to step back sometimes and not jump in when we're not really needed. This is hard for the average parent, much less the parents of the allergic kids. But at some point, we really do have to trust that our children can take care of themselves, and we've taught them well.

As long as we communicate with the school, teach our children to communicate with a trusted adult at the school, and keep the lines of communication open with our children, this will go a long way in keeping our allergic kids safe. I always say those of us with food allergies and diseases are taking a risk when we walk out of the safety of our own homes, and that is true. As Hurley points out, "You can't 'bully proof' your child, but you can teach your child the art of assertiveness, and you can create an action plan with your child so that he knows exactly what to do if bullying occurs." Now, that's some solid parenting. Go pat yourself on the back for taking care of all this and enjoy a cold one of whatever you might enjoy cold. Hint: I've just spiked my Pom-Orange Sparkly Punch (see page 158) with bourbon. Try that, and relax for a minute.

There is a fine line between being the boy who cried "bully" and nipping unacceptable behavior in the bud. My daughter declares that her brother is bullying her every time he begs her to stop singing, "It's the Hard-Knock Life." That's not bullying, that's just self-protection, my friends. The point is, all of this bullying awareness is great, but it's not always the correct accusation. As the allergic, and the parents to the allergic, we always have to be the reasonable ones in the room. Even when we want to enter a Chuck E. Cheese's with a firehose and not let our kid step foot in the Ticket Blaster until everything has been powerwashed, we must not give into that temptation. While my instinct would be to hide out in the bushes during recess and grab the kid who told mine that "gluten is a made-up allergy," that would put me in jail, thus lessening the chances that my kid will have a safe, allergy-free lunch. Bullying is never acceptable, but we cannot stamp out all of the asshats on Earth who are lacking in social skills and upset our kids. What we can do is teach our kids to be confident, vocal, and self-protective.

To recap: Talk, talk, talk to your kid and make sure he is comfortable talking to you. Talk to your kid's friends, talk to their parents, and keep talking no matter how annoying. And when it's too much, call in reinforcements from the school, your family, your friends, or whoever can be the best possible help.

Chapter

4

The Randoms: Vegan, Kosher, FODMAP, and More

would be remiss in writing a book about the eating issues of kids and the parents who feed them without throwing in a number of other nonallergic type food things that may come up at your next playdate. I have a friend with a severe garlic and onion allergy. An administrator at my children's preschool has a spinach allergy. I've met multiple gluten-free vegans, which just makes my tongue itch, and I'm married to a man who swears he's not allergic to ALL shellfish, just some. I mean, pick a side!

What I'm trying to say is that I've officially heard it all. That is, until I heard about the FODMAP diet. But before we get into that intense food situation, let me be clear that this chapter is not about food allergies, so if your only interest is to make sure the allergic in your life are safe, you may move on. Before you do, though, I have a few questions I'd like you to answer by a show of hands. I'll pretend I can see you.

How many vegetarians do you know? Vegans? Paleo peeps? What about the observant who require kosher, glatt kosher, halal meals? If you don't know any people with at least one of these food preferences, you must live alone and never socialize, ever. Vegans are everywhere, people, and even outnumber vegetarians now, if my yoga class is any indication. I'm kind of a cranky person who prefers to stay home 6.5 out of 7 days a week, and I know multiple people who follow every one of those diets. I just never invite them all over at the same time. I'm sane like that.

While the observant and the cruelty-free eaters may feel like their diets are crucial to their health (and can make very valid arguments why this is so), we get into stickier territory when we throw in our friends who are diabetic, suffer from autoimmune diseases, have high blood pressure, or require a FODMAP diet for optimum health. Now, we're getting a little bit closer to allergy territory (especially if you want to discuss diabetes, which I do), and feeding these peeps requires a bit more care. Not unlike parents of allergic kids, parents of kids with any food restrictions that can seriously negatively affect their health are not going to feel safe unless you are 100 percent clear about their situation and your ingredients. Let's see what restrictions are in store for you when inviting over the "other" crowd.

Vegan versus Vegetarian versus Pescetarian

I kind of don't think being a vegetarian is even a thing anymore, right? I mean, if you're going for the moral high ground, you're probably going all the way at this point. Who decides they don't want to eat animals, but would, in fact, prefer leather uppers and butter all over their toast? Okay, lots of people, but still, the reason veganism is growing so much is because of the vegetarians who decided not eating animals was not enough, and they needed to ban any animal products from their lives as well. It actually makes sense, even though it makes it incredibly difficult to purchase edible bread. Please let me have some eggs in my gluten-free bread, for the love of sandwiches.

Vegetarians may eat animal products such as dairy, but never eat meat. Some vegetarians will indulge in eggs, but vegans don't even think about it. Veganism means absolutely no animals, no animal products such as milk, eggs, or any products that have dairy or anything from an animal inside. This even includes honey, which is made from bees. Being vegan is restrictive but easy to remember, because it's basically nothing that has ever been a living, breathing animal or happened to come out of an animal or living creature (like bees). I have to admit, if it were not for cheese, I could totally see the point. Jeez, I love cheese.

Oh, and the pescetarians are those people who won't eat any meat, but will eat fish. I honestly don't get this no matter how unattractive I find fish. But it certainly seems incredibly healthy. I wish I could be pescetarian, but that would require my expanding my fish repertoire beyond my comfort zone. Which is tuna, salmon, and occasionally cod and halibut. But only twice a year, unless you're talking about lox.

No matter how much it may sound like I'm making fun of people who make animal-friendly choices, please know that it's only because I'm super-envious of those people who can stick to a decision like this. I wish I could, and I admire anyone who can. Godspeed, animal-lovers. I'm thinking that you'll be on the right side of history with this.

Sugar-Free

My worst nightmare, but probably the one way of eating that would make me look, and feel, like a million bucks, sugar-free eating is possibly the healthiest thing you could ever do for your body. Way back in the late 1990s, when I first moved to New York City, I had a roommate who had a great friend who was known for procuring drugs for celebrities and who simultaneously refused to eat refined sugar. Or as she called it, white death. She was ahead of her time and also got fired from her job at NBC (drug, not sugar related), but it is now all the rage to rage against refined sugar.

Look, we all know sugar is not good for anyone. Yes, it is delicious, but it will never provide a health benefit unless that health benefit is making me incredibly happy after a horrible day. Okay, so it DOES provide a health benefit, however briefly. The point is, sugar is probably something we should never eat, but that is not realistic because it is so yummy. Still, you're going to run into a parent who bans sugar, and you're going to want to know how to deal. You should also know that there is a difference in the variety of "sugar" moms.

Since diabetes runs in my family, I've always been warned about the negative health effects of sugar. When I was diagnosed with celiac disease, I decided that I took after that side of the family, and not the diabetic side, and therefore stuffing gluten-free cake into my mouth would no longer be cause for concern. Then, I learned how celiac disease and diabetes could present together, and I thought again.

Additionally, I have a friend who has a child who has such a violent reaction when she eats sugar that it has made me realize that one doesn't always have to have the diagnosis of diabetes to have a negative physical reaction when sugar is consumed. Dammit.

Sugar is complicated, and I love it like that depressed boyfriend who only wears black, even to bed. You may be ingesting sugar even when you think you're eating healthy. Fruit is certainly healthy and can contain as much as 13 grams of sugar per serving (thanks, delicious grapes!). Even though it is naturally occurring, fruit can still have a negative effect on the avoiding-sugar-for-health-reasons crowd. During my cooking experiments, I felt pretty good about creating Paleo-friendly options, and then realized that sugar is sugar is sugar. While natural is better than refined, you should know that substituting honey, maple syrup, or anything your Aunt Martha sent over for your constipation will still devolve into sugar. It's kind of not fair, as my 8-year-old self would say. Repeatedly.

What I'm trying to say is this: If you're making a meal and someone asks about the sugar content, get some specifics about her situation. Even diabetics aren't completely sugar-free; they moderate their diets and also test their blood sugar and make sure it stays within the normal range. You need to know if the sugar-free diet is a smart health goal (which means it's not on you to make sure everybody sticks to their diets) or it's a serious health issue. Other reasons one might try a sugar-free diet include a negative or allergic reaction to sugar. Before you start pulling out the stevia, know what you're dealing with and plan accordingly. Also, ask the sugar-free friends to suggest options, and/or bring a few dishes to keep everyone happy.

Honestly, I don't know what I'd do without adding sugar to my gluten- and dairy-free treats, which is why, if I'm trying to keep it healthy, I focus on serving whole foods including fruits, proteins, and vegetables. But, yeah, all fruit raises your blood sugar level, so . . . again, talk to the people in need. CRAP. SUGAR.

Kosher (Style, *Glatt,* Strict)

Unless you're Jewish and practice *kashrut* in your own home, you are not going to know what the heck is going on when your kid's friend asks if you keep kosher. Even those of us who have kids in a Jewish day school can trip up if we were not raised in a strict kosher household, so let me break it down for you. As much as I can, given that I was raised in a Protestant home in the Bible Belt, married a Jew, and am raising my kids in a Jewish fashion, which means the oldest has already told me she's an atheist. #religionfail

In Hebrew, *kosher* translates to "fit" or "proper," which makes sense when using it to describe how observant Jews must eat according to Jewish law. You must eat properly, my friends. And properly eating kosher, in general, means that only certain meats are allowed, including beef, lamb, and goat. No pork is allowed on a kosher diet, only animals that are "cloven hoofed" and "chew the cud." Additionally, meat that is eaten and has been determined kosher by a rabbi must be unblemished, not diseased, and the animal must have been killed by a ritual slaughterer who takes care to not cause the animal pain. After the animal has died, certain parts are removed that are also forbidden to eat, if you are following a stringent kosher diet. While it may be difficult to find a kosher butcher in your neighborhood, if you are hosting someone who needs it, they will certainly know where to shop.

If you're dining kosher style, there are a few things to keep in mind. Forbidden foods (*treif*) include shellfish (only fish with fins and scales are okay to eat); pork; certain birds that you would not normally have at your dinner table anyway such as stork, swan, and pelican; and wine that is bottled with casein or gelatin (wine and grape juice must be kosher). Most important, mixing milk and meat is forbidden. When I'm packing my kids' lunch boxes, I follow the no-mixing-milk-and-meat rule, and I don't throw any shellfish or pork in there. This is satisfying to their school and easy for me to remember. All of these other options can be crazy-making, and if you're hosting, it's unlikely that someone who is stringently kosher would accept anyway. It's not because your house isn't good enough, it's because kosher laws also demand that your serving ware, flatware, and cookware remain segregated as well. You cannot serve a meal that mixes meat and milk, and you cannot serve meat and milk on the same plates, using the same utensils. Since the nonobservant or non-Jewish among us don't generally have two full sets of dishes (one for meat, one for dairy), someone who is strict is not going to come over to your house and lick your *treif*-y plates.

All of this is to say, if you do have a kiddo who is eating kosher style, just skip the meat or dairy, and make sure to put the bacon away before any sleepovers. You wouldn't believe the number of cheese pizzas my kids have eaten at birthday parties. It's epic.

Glatt kosher is something you may see at a grocery store in a heavily pop-ulated Jewish neighborhood, but it is not likely to come up in conversation unless you are part of an observant community. Still, I wondered about the difference when I was looking for kosher beef, so now I know and will share it with you. *Glatt* is a Yiddish word, which means "smooth," and in this con-text, refers to the lungs of animals that are eaten, such as cows. So, if the cow had any adhesions or damage to its lungs (or other body parts), the meat is no longer kosher glatt. Without getting into the reasons why this doesn't apply to fowl, let me just state that the term *glatt* is more commonly used to describe food that is held to a higher standard.

Depending on what part of the country you live in, you may have seen endcaps at your grocery store sprout up in the spring with signs saying, "Kosher for Passover" atop a big pile of matzo. This is another layer of kosher, which, unless someone has asked you to prepare a Passover Seder, you don't need to know about. And if someone is asking you to prepare a Seder, I'm hoping you're Jewish, otherwise it's a lot to learn, and not even the best of the Jewish food holidays. (In my opinion. I have friends who claim it is the best, but I think latkes trump charoset any day. Any. Day.) The one big benefit of the kosher for Passover products is that they are generally gluten-free, with some exceptions. During Passover, leavened bread is forbidden, and so are any products containing wheat, barley, rye, oats, or spelt. You can see why just going gluten-free during Passover makes this much easier to handle.

So now you know way more than you need to know about kosher, but it will explain some of the labeling you see at the store, and help you understand my lunch-box trials.

Halal

Not dramatically different from kosher, *halal* refers to the preparation of meat and cleanliness of food, but most definitely from a different religion. Halal is common in communities with a significant Muslim population. Not unlike the ritual slaughter done by rabbis, in order for meat to be halal certified, the animal must be facing Mecca, have its throat cut while still alive, and then ritually sacrificed by a Muslim who recites a prayer dedicating the slaughter to Allah. The blood must completely empty the body before the animal is certified halal.

Halal meat is restricted to beef, lamb, goat, and birds that are not birds of prey. Eating halal means that no carnivorous animals can be eaten, nor pig, nor any food that has any products from these forbidden foods. Alcohol is also forbidden, and any food that contains blood. As *halal* means "lawful," the term describes food that is permitted and prepared according to Islamic law. Again, if you have people coming over for dinner, and they only eat halal meat, they will know where to find the proper butcher locally.

FODMAP

A recent food situation on the scene, FODMAPs are being blamed for a whole host of stomach problems. In fact, after my husband read about the health issues that could be associated with the forbidden foods on the FODMAP diet he promptly texted me, "FODMAPS are my bitch. LOL." He might not have said the LOL.

For people who have chronic digestive pain and other issues, the newest enemy in the fight for tummy freedom are foods that fall under the following categories: fermentable, oligosaccharides, disaccharides, monosaccharides, and polyols. Yeah. So let's just call them FODMAP. Onions and garlic are the biggest no-no's on a low-FODMAP diet and are blamed for causing FOD-MAPers' pain. Even small doses are not okay for people suffering with this kind of gut imbalance. But that's only the beginning. Since just about every fruit and vegetable contains fructose, fructans, and other things I cannot pronounce, it's an incredibly restrictive diet, and most people go for a low-FODMAP diet rather than cut everything out altogether for a no-FODMAP diet. Sugar alcohols are also a culprit along with dairy, loads of vegetables, and grains. If I listed all of the high-FODMAP foods here, it might get me to my word count much more quickly, but it would also take up way too much room, and you would fall asleep, dropping this book to the floor, and never be inspired to pick it up again.

Here's what you need to know about the FODMAP diet: If your doctor tells you to try it, you will get this huge list as well as a prescription for anti-depressants, because you'll basically be eating steak and air from now on. And if someone is coming over for dinner, he will only need steak and air, so that's an easy FODMAP meal to prepare.

Paleo

If you've been in the gluten-free world, you've heard of Paleo eating. It's primal, it's meaty, it's grain-free, and it's kind of delicious. The basic concept of the Paleo diet is that our bodies' digestive systems have not evolved as quickly as the agricultural and industrial revolution have. Therefore, to achieve optimum health, we should eat as our ancestors did: grass-fed meat, no dairy products, no grains, vegetables up the wazoo (except for starches), no legumes, limited fruit, lots of oils and fats, and absolutely no processed foods.

Another side project of the Paleo diet is the Whole30 diet made popular by the authors of *The Whole30: The 30-Day Guide to Total Health and Food Freedom,* super-in-shape couple Melissa and Dallas Hartwig. It's kind of like hard-core Paleo with a bit of "Move your ass!" I'll admit as someone who gets viciously ill by ingesting gluten, I try Paleo or the Whole30 diets after accidentally ingesting gluten, because both diets are designed to reduce inflammation in the body. And celiac disease is absolutely an inflammatory situation. So no matter how much fun I might make of people who live this life with seemingly no health reasons to do so, I do find it helps me to stay balanced when I'm way out of whack. Again, can I just tell you how I'm not a doctor? Cool.

If you're going very strict Paleo, you follow this diet to the letter, but there are a variety of ways to eat Paleo, depending on whom you're listening to on any given day. I've only once had a guest over who said he was Paleo, and since I love meat and greens, he was able to eat well. Otherwise, I think this is one of those food preferences wherein people should mostly fend for themselves. That being said, Paleo made me lose 5 pounds. So, there. And, please don't tell your kids I just said that. Body image positivity and all that.

What the Holy Hell Should I Make?!?

At this point, the discussion must veer into the practical. You can be a good host, treat-maker, or birthday cake–baker without adhering to every single food restriction on the planet. The eight main food allergens are already overwhelming. Add the rest of these to the menu, and you will never leave your kitchen again. So, use this chapter as an educational tool, rather than a must-do guide. When someone comes over and lets you know she only eats kosher-style or vegan, you'll know what that means. And then, you can choose to ask your guests if they would please bring their own vegan casserole because you're pretty sure you need cheese on everything else.

It's much easier to talk about personal responsibility when we talk about food issues that are not inherently dangerous. Even though your goal with your allergic children should be to make them self-sufficient and safe in the world, this is something you must do if you choose to follow a restricted diet, whether you're full-on Paleo or vegan. If your diet is incredibly important to you and your family—health reasons aside—it will be up to you, and not people hosting you or baking for the class, to create your own safe meals.

But, since I'm cool like that, here are a few recipes that fall under some of the above special diets.

CHOCO-COCONUT PALEO BROWNIES

While it has always confounded me that people on the Paleo diet can't eat russet potatoes but can eat chocolate, I'm not going to argue with a brownie. You shouldn't either.

PREP TIME: 10 minutes • **COOK TIME:** 30 minutes • **MAKES:** 12 brownies

1 cup almond flour

3 tablespoons cocoa powder

½ teaspoon baking soda

¼ teaspoon sea salt

3 eggs

¼ cup coconut oil

1 teaspoon vanilla extract

½ cup honey or agave

Shredded sweetened coconut (optional)

1. Preheat oven to 350°F and grease and almond flour an 8-inch square pan.

2. Whisk dry ingredients together in a large bowl.

3. Add eggs, one at a time, beating well after each addition.

4. Whisk remaining wet ingredients and mix until completely combined.

5. Pour mixture into prepared pan and bake for 30 minutes, or until a toothpick comes out clean from the center of the pan.

6. Remove from oven and immediately sprinkle brownies with coconut.

7. Cut into squares and serve.

VEGAN BREAKFAST OF CHAMPIONS

I may prefer a scramble to start my day, but you can still satisfy your morning hunger while keeping it animal- and animal-product free. One of my favorite breakfast hacks growing up was when we had leftover rice from the night before. My mom would microwave it, pour milk on it, and add a few teaspoonfuls of sugar. You can make it vegan and a bit healthier by either skipping the milk altogether or using a milk alternative, and swap out the refined sugar for a different sweet option.

PREP TIME: 2 minutes • **MAKES:** 1 serving

> 1 cup cooked rice
>
> 2 tablespoons milk (I prefer almond)
>
> 1 tablespoon maple syrup
>
> Berries, slivered almonds, sliced apples (optional)

1. Warm up rice in the microwave for 60 seconds.

2. Mix in milk and syrup.

3. Top with berries or whatever floats your boat.

MY FAVORITE KOSHER CHICKEN DINNER

Note that this is kosher-style, as in if you're going for strict kosher or glatt, make sure that the meat you buy has been cleared by a rabbi. Having prepared multiple meals, too many to count actually, in the kosher-style, this is my guide. If you are strict kosher or glatt kosher, please talk to your butcher and/or rabbi before eating. But I'm guessing you already knew that.

I also call this Sunday Chicken because it's such a staple in our house at the beginning of the week, and I know the leftovers will go far. Far enough to put into my children's kosher-style lunch boxes.

PREP TIME: 15 minutes • **COOK TIME:** 1½ hours • **MAKES:** 8 servings

> 1–5 pounds organic chicken
>
> 1½ tablespoons coconut oil, plus more for coating chicken
>
> 6 cloves garlic
>
> 1 lemon, quartered
>
> 3 cups organic chicken stock, plus more if desired
>
> 1 onion, chopped
>
> 1 pound new potatoes
>
> 4 carrots, quartered
>
> Salt and black pepper

1. Preheat oven to 400°F.

2. Coat chicken skin on top as well as underneath with coconut oil. Dice 3 cloves of garlic and place underneath chicken skin. Place the 3 remaining whole garlic cloves and lemon inside chicken cavity. Pour stock into roasting pan and cover bottom of pan with onions.

3. Roast for approximately 1½ hours, flipping the bird over halfway through cooking time. Baste chicken periodically with chicken stock. Add water, if necessary.

4. While the chicken is roasting, place potatoes and carrots on a large baking sheet and cover with coconut oil. Lightly salt and pepper. Add a splash of chicken stock for flavor, if desired. Roast vegetables for 40 minutes.

5. Using a meat thermometer, check after 1 hour to see if temperature has reached 165°F. If not, continue cooking until the internal temperature reaches 165°F.

6. Allow chicken to rest for 10 minutes after removing from oven, then serve with vegetables.

CHICKEN & QUINOA SALAD FOR THE FODMAP CROWD

Again, this is low-FODMAP, so not everything in this mix is free of all FODMAPs. It is, however, very low in those irritants and very high on the yummy scale.

PREP TIME: 15 minutes • **COOK TIME:** 30 minutes • **MAKES:** 6 servings

½ cup quinoa

8 ounces skinless, boneless chicken breast, cut into 1"–2" pieces

1 tablespoon wheat-free tamari

Juice of half a lime

Salt and black pepper

3 tablespoons extra-virgin olive oil

12 ounces green beans, trimmed and cut into 1½" pieces

2 cups cooked corn kernels

1 tablespoon minced fresh marjoram

½ teaspoon coarse kosher salt

1. Prepare quinoa according to instructions, and allow to cool. Marinate chicken in tamari, lime juice, salt, and pepper.

2. Heat 1 tablespoon oil in heavy medium skillet over medium-high heat. Add chicken to skillet; cook until golden brown and cooked through, about 8 minutes.

3. Cook green beans in large saucepan of boiling salted water until tender-crisp, about 4 minutes. Drain. Rinse under cold water to cool; drain. Transfer beans to kitchen towel and pat dry.

4. Mix quinoa, chicken, green beans, and corn in large bowl.

5. Combine remaining 2 tablespoons oil, marjoram, and kosher salt in small bowl.

6. Pour over salad and toss to coat. Season, to taste, with salt and pepper. Serve.

RASPBERRY-LIME SELTZER

I grew up in the 1980s in the middle of the country, so when New York seltzer was brought to our town, I was IN. Actually living in New York City made me commit to seltzer drinking for a lifetime, which is why the best way to serve up fun drinks without sugar involves the bubbly water that makes kids happy. While you can squeeze whatever fruits in that will make your little ones believe water is a treat, my kids love this lime and raspberry combo, and I do too.

PREP TIME: 1 minute • MAKES: 2 drinks

> 12 ounces seltzer
> ½ cup raspberries, muddled
> Juice of 1 lime

1. With a long spoon, mix seltzer, raspberries, and lime juice well.

2. Serve over ice. Enjoy.

Note: I am now going to admit to you that I created this beverage while working as a bartender in a Manhattan hotel when I was also watching my weight and very sweaty due to a particularly hot summer. So, if you want to create the adult version, skip the raspberries in the recipe and add a shot of Stoli Razberi Vodka. Just make sure to keep it away from the kiddos, and remember that alcohol does equal sugar.

The last word on all of this has to do with your own personal threshold for socializing and food. I love having get-togethers, and I love to cook up fun eats for everyone. I will fully admit to many missteps in the past, as I like to experiment (hence, this whole cookbook gig), and I like to try to make people happy given any food issues that are present. Still, sometimes, you're just too knackered to deal and want to sit on your back porch and throw back some drinks without having to constantly check the pudding. These are the best times, and the moments when you demand a potluck where everyone brings what they want to eat, and you provide the beverages. Fun will ensue, and no one will go home hungry.

Mazel!

Chapter

5

Kitchen Boot Camp

For those of you who are facing a lifetime of cooking allergen-free, yet have never learned the difference between a Cutie (clementine) and a Halo (mandarin) this chapter is for you. (Also, it doesn't really matter what the difference is, as long as your kid will eat them.) For those of you who just want to have some safe snacks when your daughter's allergic BFF comes over, you will learn a little something about getting your kitchen into shape with this chapter, but I totally get it if you're like, "Just tell me what to buy, already!!!" (See Resources on page 197.)

Cooking can be a little intimidating for the uninitiated, but with a few tricks and even more great recipes, you'll be the kitchen champ in no time. Hell, even if you only perfect one recipe that's appropriate for your nephew with a peanut allergy, that's pretty dang good, too. Remember, we're all doing the best we can, and no one expects perfection. The only thing that must be perfect is the safety of your kitchen. The cooking part can be sloppy, weird, messy, and fun.

A note about cooking, in general. Some people call cooking an art, others call it a science. While it certainly can help you teach your kiddos about science and math, and some recipes in baking require greater precision than others, I fall into the "art" camp. I grew up with two grandmothers who just whipped food together without recipes. The rest of us had to try and figure out what they were doing, exactly, so we could repeat the delicious dishes in our own kitchens. Which is how I come to so many recipes you'll find in this book: experimenting, and messing up. You, too, can play around in the kitchen with safe ingredients until you find your perfect allergy-free cookie. Once you have the general idea of how ingredients work together (this is also the science part), you can create whatever you're craving. Don't be afraid to try something new, try something ridiculous, or try something you just had in a restaurant and don't want to pay $50 for again. Get your hands dirty, but keep your food clear of allergens. Go have fun!

Intimidation in the Spice Aisle

A big part of cooking allergy-friendly is the removal of certain foods from your home. If you have a severe allergy, or sometimes even if it's mild, you'll want to take that allergen, kick it to the curb, and spray bleach on any surfaces it encountered. It's totally like that scene in *Silkwood* but with gluten/dairy/egg/soy/tree nuts/peanuts/fish/shellfish. While you'll be armed with your notes from your pediatrician, allergist, or nutritionist about what foods you have to forcibly remove, now is the time we're going to talk about what foods you CAN have and will need.

Before you head to the store for your weekly groceries, add these pantry items to the list, so you'll have great ingredients on hand when you feel like you have no idea what to put in Sigmund's lunch box anymore. This, along with those snacks, can go a long way when you just can't deal with the gluten-free crêpe sandwiches anymore.

Stock These

All-purpose gluten-free, dairy-free flour

Baking powder

Baking soda

Black, pinto, or white beans

Black pepper

Brown sugar

Butter, or ghee if you're
lactose-free, Earth Balance if
you're dairy-free/vegan

Cinnamon

Corn tortillas

Cornstarch

Dairy-free, soy-free, good-quality
chocolate

Dairy-free cocoa powder

Egg substitutes such as Ener-G or
golden flaxseeds (see Chapter 7)

Fresh favorite fruits

Fresh favorite vegetables

Garlic

Ginger, fresh or powdered

Gluten-free pasta (look for other
allergens such as eggs and dairy)

Herbs, fresh or dried

Hummus

Lemons or other citrus fruits

Lentils

Milk or milk alternative

Nonprocessed meats

Nutmeg

Olive oil

Onions

Potatoes

Powdered sugar

Quinoa

Red-pepper flakes

Rice

Rice crackers

Sea salt

Sugar or sugar substitute

SunButter or Hippie Butter

Tomatoes or tomato sauce

Vanilla extract

Vegetable oil

Wheat-free tamari or coconut
aminos

You're going to find it much easier to whip up a meal or two if you have everything you need on hand and much easier to fake it when you have ingredients that can work together in a pinch.

This Recipe Makes Me Itch

The recipes in this book are written so that you can get down to the business of making kid-friendly, allergy-friendly foods quickly. While some are more complicated than others (gluten-free, dairy-free, cream-filled cupcakes,

FTW!), the idea is to be able to feed the allergic kiddos in your house easily and well. I'm including these kitchen tips so that you can have a leg up when you get inspired to create cupcake bowls, and so you'll know your way around that oven. Make that oven your bitch, people. Do it. Always:

- Preheat the oven for at least 20 minutes.

- Remember to use all-purpose gluten-free, dairy-free flour for rolling out dough, greasing, and flouring a pan, and any other place where you need to keep it gluten- and dairy-free.

- Chill cookie dough for at least 30 minutes before shaping and baking.

- Bring eggs (if you're using them) to room temperature before mixing.

- Test a recipe before you try it out on guests or for holidays.

- Have a nonallergic friend try your baked goods before sharing with others. You need a second opinion for new recipes.

- Cook with olive oil, and make salad dressings and dips with extra-virgin olive oil. Regular olive oil is better for heat, and extra-virgin is better for dressings and cool dishes.

- Make your own allergy-free dish and bring it to the party. You don't know what is going on in other people's kitchens.

- Check baked goods for doneness with a toothpick or sharp knife. Ovens differ in settings, and altitude makes recipes wonky.

- Eat allergy-free baked goods quickly, or freeze. The shelf life of allergy-free homemade baked goods is not as long as for the regular ones.

- Experiment with gluten-free, soy-free, nut-free, dairy-free flours. Everything from millet to mesquite is on the market now, so enjoy testing them all in your favorite brownie recipe.

- Try a recipe again, and tweak it if your gut tells you that it needs something a little bit different.

- Keep your pots, pans, bakeware, cutting boards, and rolling pins allergy-free as well.

- Cook gluten-free, egg-free pastas to al dente. They can get blobby if they overcook, and nobody wants that.

- Have ingredients on hand to make your kiddo's favorite recipe. A hard day at a birthday party can be made better when he comes home to his very own allergy-free cupcakes.

As long as you have checked the ingredients list for allergens, never feel guilty about using pre-made cheats in your recipes. Your cooking requirements are hard enough already.

Naturally, when you're purchasing prepared foods, you must know what every ingredient is to ensure that it is truly allergy-free. The brands I use are gluten-free (see Resources on page 197), but you will certainly find other brands at your local grocery stores. Don't forget to read the fine print when you're picking out your pre-made cheats, because I feel the need to remind you of this five million times. Look for:

- Allergy-friendly snacks (see Resources on page 197)

- Bagged, prewashed greens

- Barbecue sauce (check for gluten-free and soy-free)

- Frozen allergy-free meals when you're just not able to cook (see Resources on page 197)

- Frozen herbs and garlic

- Frozen rice

- Gluten-free, dairy-free pancake and waffle mix

- Marinara sauce

- Precooked lentils and beans

- Pre-made gluten-free, dairy-free pie crust

- Pre-made gluten-free, egg-free pasta

- Pre-made polenta (make sure it's gluten-free—not all of them are)

- Ranch dressing (vegan version for egg- and dairy-free diets)

- Spray canola oil, but make sure it doesn't have added flour

- Spray olive oil

Shopping Spree at Sur La Table!

A shopping spree is what I'd do if someone said, "Welp, you gotta go buy new stuff so you can cook like a champ in an allergy-free kitchen!" Or I'd go to Target, actually, since that's more in line with my budget. Still, it's exciting to fantasize as you walk by those display windows at Sur La Table, am I right? Or, maybe that's just their free samples of Nespresso talking. Either way, you'll need some stuff when you decide to get serious in the kitchen. Some items are more necessary than others, and, as you begin to cook more and experiment, you'll figure out what you need and what you can skip. While I love having a dough cutter, a stand mixer, and other one-trick-pony gadgets (pizza scissors, anyone?), you really can get by with the basics. Of course, I call an ice-cream maker a basic . . . just so you know.

Kitchen Tools You'll Want and Need

8- or 9-inch round cake pans (3)

9-by-13-inch baking pans (2)

Baking sheets (2)

Blender or food processor

Box grater

Can opener

Candy thermometer

Casserole dishes in varying sizes (3)

Cast-iron skillet (1)

Dutch oven

Full set of dishes

Full set of knives (including bread knife)

Hand grater

Hand juicer

Hand masher

Hand mixer

Kitchen shears

Knife sharpener

Ladle

Large roasting pan

Liquid measuring cup

Loaf pan

Mandoline

Measuring cups

Measuring spoons

Meat tenderizer

Meat thermometer

Metal whisks (2)

Microplane

Mixing bowls in varying sizes (6)

Mixing spoons (2 large)

Muffin tins (2)

Pizza cutter

Pizza pan

Salad bowl

Salad spinner

Saucepans (1 small, 1 medium, and 1 large)

Serving spoons

Sifter

Skillets (1 small, 1 medium, and 1 large)

Slotted spoon

Spatulas (2 plastic, 1 metal)

Strainers (1 large and 1 small)

Timer

Toaster oven

Tongs

Vegetable peeler

Thoughts on Flours

What's Up with Cake Flour?

I've been using a cookbook from the infamous Magnolia Bakery of New York City for at least 15 years. While I used to whip up goodies before my celiac diagnosis, I gave up after because of the need for cake flour in their recipes. While I finally found a gluten-free cake flour (Steve's GF Cake Flour by Authentic Foods!!!), I have also discovered that you can use multi-purpose Cup4Cup gluten-free flour. I'm going for it, and you should, too. But remember, Cup4Cup has dairy, so if you need dairy-free flour, search out the Authentic Foods version. It works so well that the pros are using it to make amazing commercial cupcakes.

The Flour Will Rise Again

Another item you frequently see in recipes is self-rising flour. Again, I thought those days were over once I had to use my gluten-free flours, but it turns out that you just need a little tweaking to make your all-purpose, gluten-free, dairy-free flour self-rising. Here's the recipe.

PREP TIME: 1 minute • **MAKES:** 1 cup

> 1 cup all-purpose gluten-free, dairy-free flour
>
> 1 teaspoon baking powder
>
> ¼ teaspoon salt

Whisk ingredients together, and that's your self-rising flour!

Gums and Such

Some flours, like King Arthur Flour gluten-free, dairy-free, suggest using xanthan gum in their recipes. I don't know if it's the climate I live in or the nature of the recipes, but I've never missed it in my recipes. If you're having trouble getting dough to stick together, however, try a small amount of xanthan gum to see if you can't improve on what you're baking. You can also try guar gum or arrowroot, if that's more to your liking. They all have the same goal, which is to make your gluten-free versions behave more like those with gluten.

Baking versus Cooking

Back when I ate without any restrictions whatsoever, I had my all-purpose flour ready to go whether I was making cookies or fried chicken. Given the expense of gluten-free flours, I've adjusted my flour usage, and if you'd like to save money, you should follow my example. Certain flours make baked goods delectable (Cup4Cup and Better Batter), and I always reach for those when I'm trying to make something seem like it's neither gluten- nor dairy-free. But if I'm re-creating mozzarella sticks, I don't need the light and fluffy stuff to surround my melted cheese. I usually have a less expensive option available for cooking, and for recipes that call for a tiny amount of flour, rather than a baked good that depends on the fluffy stuff.

Chapter
6

Let's Talk about Lunch

Now that we're all clear on what is making kids sick in the America, I'm guessing that you all want to know what in the heck we CAN send to school that won't offend the senses. And those of you who are dealing with a food allergy in your house are probably tired of the same old, same old in a brown paper bag. This is the part where I give you delicious recipes, and you get to change up the lunch routine for your little eaters. Hooray!

But first, let's monitor the school-provided lunch for any options on those days when you just cannot cut up another carrot stick. For kids with severe allergies, you probably won't want to risk any cross-contact with the allergen and will continue to pack a lunch. So, your goal here is to teach your child how to prepare his own packed lunch so you can leave this task behind at some point before you lose your ever-loving mind.

Whether you're packing lunch or buying it, it is incredibly important to educate your allergic kid, so she will be able to fend for herself when you are not around. This is quite possibly a lifelong situation for your little one, and she'll need to understand the importance of vigilance while eating, as well as her own physical reactions, in order to keep herself safe and healthy for a lifetime. It may seem like a lot to ask of your kids, and for some of them, it could be, but you must start early and continue to reiterate the facts of her food allergy until she's all, "Mo-o-o-o-om, I get it! I'm not a baby, stop treating me like one!" Only then will you know you have succeeded.

So, the lunchroom! While most schools offer a hot lunch option, many options are not exactly healthy for our growing kiddos. I was lucky to grow up in a very small school, where the head cook was, indeed, a gourmet. And having to only prepare food for a small population helped her to stretch the school budget and provide some healthy and delicious options for us. You may have a similar situation, or at least a small enough school where you can talk to the kitchen staff, and they will always have a clear idea of the ingredients going into the school lunch. If that's the case, then begin by meeting with the school to discuss your child's allergy. Ask for a weekly menu so you can review it with the kitchen staff, and then explain the options to your child. Ideally, this would morph into an independent discussion between your child and whoever is serving up Salisbury steak. The point being, the staff will get used to understanding, and communicating, what exactly is going into the lunch items, and your child will be able to understand what is safe and what is not. You can see why so many of us opt to just make our own damn lunches, yes?

While the lunchroom discussion is a great way to start teaching your child about having all of these conversations to ensure her health while dining out, it is also a lot to ask of a kid who can easily be distracted by a wicked game of handball happening outside as soon as everyone Hoovers up their lunches. You know your kid, and you know how much, or how little, you have to do to keep her safe. Whether you decide that navigating the school lunch is worth the risk or not, it's still a great idea to have your child learn how to decipher food and learn what ingredients go into those pizza squares, exactly.

The Future of the Cafeteria

In spite of living in the middle of the world's largest suburb, my kids also go to a small school. A school so small that until this past year, there wasn't even a formal school-lunch program. The excitement in our household when we received the email telling us that those days of packed lunches were over was unparalleled. Since both of my children are now allergy-free, I signed them up as quickly as I could say, "No more zip-top plastic bags!!!!" After my husband and I finished our happy dance, we sat down to order our kids' lunches online, and that's when I noticed that there was a button you could push to choose the "gluten-free" option and, in some cases, such as on sandwich day, you could choose "kosher" if you wanted your lunchmeat to be from a kosher deli or butcher. (It's a Jewish day school, so the style was already kosher. See Chapter 4 for more details on the difference.) I also saw a vegan pizza option alongside the regular pizza, and that's when I realized that something different might be going on at my kids' school. It became fully realized when I picked up my son early for a doctor's appointment, and I caught him mid-lunch. It turns out that, in addition to the regular hot lunch, there was a stocked salad bar with specialty items such as hummus and pita, so kids had a wide variety of options. I also took a whiff of the chicken-and-rice bowls, and got instantly hungry. I realize that this is not something that ever happens in a school cafeteria after the age of 18, but what they were cooking up smelled damn good. When I saw that the teachers and administrators were also enjoying the hot lunch, I had to ask the principal what was up with this lunch situation. She agreed that it smelled amazing and explained that it was because the team used all fresh ingredients in the hot lunch, and it was, in fact, delicious. She then went on to tell me that it was also eight main allergen-free.

What the . . . ?

Naturally, I tracked down the guy in charge of this lunchroom madness and begged him to talk to me and explain the magic that was the hot lunch at my kids' school. Chef John J. Bard is a certified executive chef and the culinary director of Wilshire Boulevard Temple Hospitality and has been preparing the food for the WBT camps of Hilltop and Hess Kramer in Malibu ever since becoming a parent himself. As a chef, Bard realized that the lifestyle that usually goes along with running a restaurant kitchen was not conducive to being a parent and fell into the "kid realm" of summer camps. Bard was already looking into cooking "clean," using only a few ingredients, when landing a job at a camp that already had the restriction of kosher eating inspired him to make a better quality of food for kids. As he explained to me, "There are already restrictions with Judaism, and so that takes out shellfish, dairy if you're serving meat, and that easily leads to cooking in a vegan style."

Bard goes the extra mile here, as he is incredibly conscientious about removing the eight main allergens or providing options for those who need them. "It's a life-or-death situation sometimes, so I want to make kids feel as comfortable as possible when they're eating my food," Bard explains. "I don't want them to feel singled out, and that makes all the difference." So, beyond the cooking cleanly, Bard also makes sure that the kids who have food restrictions are not forced to eat at separate times, at separate tables, or otherwise pointed out to the rest of the crowd. Yes, I wanted to hug him, too.

Since Bard has been working with kids for so long, he knows that the most important part of the equation to feeding kids safely is the parental anxiety. His way of making the kids and parents feel safe while also not feeling weird or left out is twofold: (1) calm the parents down, and (2) make the kids feel comfortable. He certainly made me feel safe as he explained how his staff of 32 at three facilities and his 12 to 15 chefs go about making the allergy-friendly menus.

Bard has his staff take the FDA online course in allergy safety. While he doesn't cook with peanuts or tree nuts at all, and since shellfish is not kosher, that's off the menu as well, he does use dairy and gluten, but has a special area where gluten-free food is prepared. They are ready for any allergy restriction by following these rules and utilizing colored cutting boards, knives, and other food-prep tools. Additionally, when you're using very few ingredients, you can make menu changes easily. (He has a nut-free, gluten-free oatmeal and maple syrup granola that the kids go crazy for at the schools, and at the camps.)

At the end of the day, Bard explains that he really wants to help kids to not be afraid of food, even if they have food allergies. "I take it seriously, and I get great satisfaction out of doing it," he told me as I gushed over him and declared that he was basically the best chef in the entire universe, ever.

Lucky for my kids and their classmates, Bard has expanded into preparing food for kids year-round with two elementary schools and preschools in Los Angeles to keep him and his staff busy 12 months of the year. When I asked him if he knew about any other chefs preparing food for schools in this way, he did not. I haven't heard of this, either, but I am hoping this is the wave of the future. Not just for our food-allergic kids, but as a healthier way of feeding kids who eat one or two meals away from home every day. Imagine the difference a healthy, thoughtful, fresh, unprocessed diet could make in every kid's life. While the students who go to school with mine are obviously the luckiest children in the entire world, I have to wonder, if our school can manage this, why not more? Before everyone flips me the bird, let me just say that I KNOW why this isn't possible, and the answer is money. It's always money, isn't it? Still, I did suggest Bard take this show on the road and train school chefs around the country, so our kids could be healthy and safe. I'm waiting to see if Bard starts a revolution. Fingers crossed.

In the meantime, here are some lunch-box options for kids with allergies to enjoy before everyone gets inspired to think about what goes into hot lunches in schools around the world. That's going to happen, right?

LUNCH-BOX FAVORITES

Here's where I admit that I have lots of Mexican-inspired recipes in the lunch-box section. This is for many reasons; the most obvious being that Mexican food is delicious. It also happens to be very allergen-friendly, easy to make, and a kid favorite no matter what meal we're talking about. Easy to pack, easy to stack, here are your new lunch-box favorites.

Key

Gluten (G), Dairy (D), Peanuts (P), Tree Nuts
(TN), Soy (S), Egg (E), Fish (F), and Shellfish
(SF)—means it is free of these allergens.

VEGAN HOT DOG BUNS
G, D, P, TN, S, E, F, SF (8/8)

I say the easiest way to fill up a lunch box is to start off with a safe roll and just start stuffing. I made this roll for CNBC's reality show *Restaurant Startup* when a vegan hot dog joint was looking for a gluten-free roll to match. You will need a hot dog mold to make the perfect bun, or you can try and free-hand it by rolling it into a hot dog shape and placing it in an aluminum foil boat that is also hot dog shaped. It's a zillion times easier to use the mold, so if you plan on making this your go-to roll, invest in that fun cooking tool and start making hot dog Jell-O or the like in your downtime. Note that the sesame seeds are optional, and you need to be aware that sesame seeds can be an allergen, so if you're making these buns for a large group, just skip that particular accoutrement.

PREP TIME: 15 minutes + 1 hour rise time • COOK TIME: 20 minutes • MAKES: 8 buns

 2 tablespoons flax meal

 6 tablespoons plus 1 cup warm water

 3½ cups all-purpose gluten-free and dairy-free flour

 ¼ cup tapioca starch

 1 teaspoon kosher salt

2½ teaspoons active dry yeast (not the quick rise)

2 tablespoons maple syrup

¼ cup olive oil

1 teaspoon apple-cider vinegar

Canola oil

Sesame seeds (optional)

1. Make egg substitute by mixing flax meal with 6 tablespoons warm water and allowing to stand while you prepare the rest of the dough.

2. Combine flour, tapioca starch, and kosher salt in large mixing bowl made for a stand. Set aside.

3. Allow yeast to bloom by combining yeast, remaining 1 cup warm water, and syrup in small bowl. Let stand for 7 minutes exactly.

4. Using a paddle attachment, mix egg substitute, ¼ cup water, oil, and vinegar to dry ingredients and just combine. Add bloomed yeast mixture and mix on a medium setting for 2 minutes, or until completely combined.

5. Prepare a hot dog or other bun pan by coating with oil. Divide dough evenly among 8 molds. Using wet hands, smooth the batter on top. Sprinkle sesame seeds on top, if desired. Allow dough to rise for 1 hour.

6. Preheat oven to 375°F. Bake for 20 minutes, or until golden brown.

7. Remove buns and allow to cool. Split open and throw a dawg in there.

PIE CRUST

G, D, P, TN, S, E, F, SF (8/8) Vegan

Personally, I grab a gluten-free pie crust from Whole Foods, or whip up a mix from a gluten-free pie crust box (see Resources on page 197). But, depending on your allergy issues, you'll want to have a recipe on hand to keep everyone safe. This can be used for so many different recipes, as you'll see below, and will become your best friend. While you can make this crust well ahead and allow to chill in your fridge for a few days, remember that gluten-free and dairy-free crust is not nearly as stable as traditional crust. I recommend using it right away or within 24 hours. Yes, it will surely still break apart at times, but that's the cross we must bear in order to enjoy safe and delicious baked goods once again.

As always, check gluten-free all-purpose flour mix to make sure that it's dairy-free (see Resources on page 197). Of course, if you're not using gluten-free flour, it will be naturally dairy-free.

PREP TIME: 7 minutes • **CHILL TIME:** 30 minutes or up to 24 hours
COOK TIME: 15 minutes to lightly brown (check recipe) • **MAKES:** 2 pie crusts

> 3 cups all-purpose gluten-free and dairy-free flour
>
> ¼ cup sugar
>
> 1 teaspoon salt
>
> ½ cup Earth Balance Soy-Free Natural Buttery Spread, chilled
>
> ¼ cup vegetable shortening
>
> 2 teaspoons apple-cider vinegar
>
> ½ cup cold water

1. Using an electric hand mixer or a stand mixer, combine dry ingredients. Add Earth Balance and shortening to dry ingredients and mix well. Mixture will be crumbly.

2. Add vinegar and water and mix until the dough begins to form.

3. Remove ball of dough from mixer, knead with hands, and form a ball. Place on parchment paper, and allow to chill for ½ hour.

4. Remove from refrigerator and separate into 2 balls. Roll out into disks about ⅛" thick for pie crusts, or rectangles ⅛" thick for hand pies or tarts.

5. Bake according to recipe.

RICE CHEX CHICKEN FINGERS

G, D, P, TN, E, F, SF (7/8)

Kids love chicken fingers, but finding breadcrumbs that are gluten-, egg-, and dairy-free is a huge challenge. Rice Chex and other Chex products (see Resources on page 197) are seven main allergen-free, so you can use them to crunch up your salads or coat your fried chicken. Keep it dairy- and nut-free by using rice milk in this recipe, but if you can have the dairy, thicker milk works well.

PREP TIME: 20 minutes • **COOK TIME:** 15 minutes • **MAKES:** 12 servings

2 pounds boneless chicken breasts or thighs

4 cups Rice Chex

1 teaspoon salt

1 teaspoon black pepper

1 teaspoon paprika

1 cup rice milk

3 cups vegetable oil

Sauces for dipping (optional; check allergen info on label)

1. If not already cut into fingers, slice chicken into 6" strips, approximately 2" wide. Set aside.

2. In a food processor or blender, combine Rice Chex, salt, pepper, and paprika. Pulse until texture resembles breadcrumbs. Transfer to a large plate.

3. Pour milk into medium bowl and set up assembly line with chicken tenders, milk, and Rice Chex mixture. Place chicken tenders in bowl with milk.

4. Heat oil on medium-high heat in large skillet or use a deep-fat fryer and heat on medium-high. Once water sprinkles "dance" on the surface, the oil is ready. Turn heat down to medium.

5. Dredge milk-soaked chicken in Rice Chex mixture, coating completely.

6. Transfer to oil and cook until browned, 5 to 7 minutes per side. Allow chicken to drain on paper towel-covered plate.

7. Serve chicken tenders alone, or with sauces, if desired.

VEGAN "HOT DOGS"

G, D, P, TN, E, F, SF (7/8) Vegan

A good friend of mine is one of the owners of Fritzi Dog in Los Angeles at the Farmer's Market, where they impressed the masses by creating a vegan hot dog using carrots. While all of our minds were blown, my husband was especially impressed and demanded the recipe. No dice, but we got an idea and went about experimenting in the kitchen. While they use the sous vide style of cooking, I just throw everything into a gallon zip-top bag, because I'm not as fancy. The flavor of these "hot dogs" is really top-notch, and while you'll never fool anyone into believing this is a Hebrew National, it's still a great option to serve up at mixed-allergen parties, or to pop into your vegan kid's lunch box.

PREP TIME: 10 minutes • **CHILL TIME:** 24 hours • **COOK TIME:** 15 minutes • **MAKES:** 4 servings

> 4 large carrots, peeled, with the ends cut off
> (I cut mine to the size of the hot dog bun)
>
> ¼ cup wheat-free tamari
>
> 1 tablespoon white-wine vinegar
>
> 3 teaspoons apple-cider vinegar
>
> 1 clove garlic, minced
>
> ¼ teaspoon red-pepper flakes
>
> ½ teaspoon paprika
>
> 1 tablespoon olive oil
>
> 4 Vegan Hot Dog Buns (page 78)
>
> Mustard, ketchup, relish, onions, peppers (optional)

1. Boil 5 cups of water in a large pot and add carrots. Boil for 5 minutes.

2. While carrots are boiling, whisk together tamari, ¼ cup water, vinegars, garlic, pepper flakes, and paprika in a large bowl.

3. When carrots are done cooking, place them in a zip-top bag and add mixture on top. Seal bag, releasing as much air out of the bag as possible. Allow carrots to marinate in the refrigerator for at least 24 hours.

4. Heat oil on medium-high heat in a medium skillet for 1 to 2 minutes. Reduce heat to medium and cook carrots until warm and start to crisp— 8 to 10 minutes.

5. Remove from heat. Serve on buns with your favorite toppings, as desired.

BACON & TOMATO SOUP

G, D, P, TN, S, E, F, SF (8/8)

You can leave off the bacon and still have a delicious soup, but not as baconrrific. If you're full-on vegan, use vegetable stock instead of chicken stock, skip the bacon, and you're all set. I like to grab a gluten- and dairy-free bagel from my local vegan baker and cut it into ½" squares, cover in olive oil, sprinkle with salt and pepper, and toast it until crispy for special croutons.

PREP TIME: 20 minutes • **COOK TIME:** 1 hour • **MAKES:** 12 servings

Olive oil

4 large tomatoes, seeds removed and quartered

6 cloves garlic, chopped

¼ teaspoon salt, plus more for sprinkling

¼ teaspoon black pepper, plus more for sprinkling

2½ cups gluten-free chicken stock

1 can (15 ounces) fire-roasted tomatoes

1 large russet potato, peeled and quartered

5 slices bacon

2 tablespoons coconut milk

1. Preheat oven to 425°F.

2. Coat a baking sheet with oil. Place tomatoes and garlic on sheet and lightly salt and pepper. Bake for 35 minutes, until tomatoes are charred.

3. In a Dutch oven, combine stock, tomatoes and garlic, and canned tomatoes. Sprinkle with salt and pepper. Bring mixture to a boil and add potatoes. Turn heat to medium-low and cook for 30 minutes.

4. While the soup is cooking, fry bacon and allow to cool.

5. Remove soup from heat and blend with immersion blender until smooth. Return to heat and add coconut milk. Mix thoroughly and allow to cook for 5 minutes.

6. Crumble bacon on top of bowls of soup, add allergy-free croutons or crackers, and serve.

BACON "SUSHI"

G, D, P, TN, S, E, F, SF (8/8)

Yes, I love bacon (nonkosher, nonvegetarian, nonvegan), and kids do, too. Perfect for you bento box parents, you can mix up your sushi toppings with ham, roasted or fresh vegetables for the vegans, or even just by adding a drizzle of honey for a sweet treat. The most labor-intensive part of this recipe (the making of the sticky rice) can also be avoided by buying premade sticky rice, which is also gluten-, egg-, and dairy-free. Maybe do that, and leave yourself time for those adorable animal shapes.

PREP TIME: 2½ hours (including soaking time) • **COOK TIME:** 45 minutes
MAKES: 6 servings

> 1 cup sushi rice
> 1 teaspoon rice vinegar
> ¼ teaspoon sugar
> 3 strips bacon

1. In a medium bowl, rinse rice with water until the water is no longer cloudy. Drain water off rice and leave rice in bowl.

2. Cover rice completely with hot water and allow rice to soak for at least 2 hours.

3. Bring 2 cups of water to a boil in the bottom of a double-boiler or small pot.

4. Drain rice in a fine strainer and place the strainer over boiling water, without touching the water, cover with a lid, and steam for 30 minutes, flipping rice over halfway through. Make sure lid fits as tightly as possible.

5. Remove rice from heat and let rest for 5 minutes.

6. In a medium bowl, combine rice, vinegar and sugar. Place rice in refrigerator for 15 minutes to cool.

7. While rice is cooling, fry bacon over medium-high heat on the stovetop. Remove to a paper towel-lined plate. Cut bacon in 1" to 2" squares.

8. Remove rice from refrigerator and shape into nigiri rolls approximately 2 inches long.

9. Top rolls with bacon and pack them up for lunch.

YUM CHIPS

G, D, P, TN, S, E, F, SF (8/8)

Sweet potato to plantain, the healthy chips that parents and kids love. Go all sweet potato, or mix with carrots, parsnips, and purple 'taters for a colorful, healthy snack. While you can certainly deep-fry these and add paprika, if you want to make sure your kids won't be overwhelmed by too much flavor and grease, you can bake them, as explained below.

Plantain Tip: Use 1 tablespoon more oil, and cook at a slightly lower temperature—375°F.

PREP TIME: 15 minutes • COOK TIME: 30 minutes • MAKES: 6 servings

> 2 potatoes, sweet potatoes, yams, or plantains
> Olive oil
> Salt and black pepper

1. Preheat oven to 450°F and space racks evenly apart for best heat distribution.

2. Line 2 baking sheets with aluminum foil.

3. Slice potatoes or vegetable of choice very thin (⅛") using a mandoline, if possible, and space evenly on baking sheets.

4. Cover with oil and toss to evenly distribute. Add salt and pepper, to taste.

5. Bake for 25 to 30 minutes, stirring occasionally. Check for doneness at 25 minutes.

6. Remove chips when they are crispy on the edges. Taste for seasoning, and add more salt, if desired.

7. Serve immediately with your favorite dip or alone.

CINNAMON TOASTER TARTS

G, D, P, TN, S, F, SF (7/8)

As a kid, my favorite Pop-Tart was the cinnamon version. Even though I wasn't in the habit of enjoying them into my adulthood, I'll admit to fighting my family members for the last gluten-free, dairy-free Cinnamon Toaster Tart after I whipped these up. If you're not dairy-free or vegan, use cow milk in the glaze for a thicker, stickier glaze. This is one of the many recipes you can make easier by buying a gluten-free, dairy-free pie crust mix, or use Pie Crust (page 80). Either way, it will be the first thing your kid eats when he opens up his lunch box.

PREP TIME: 20 minutes • **COOK TIME:** 25 minutes • **MAKES:** 8 tarts

Tarts

> Pie Crust (page 80), chilled
>
> 2 teaspoons cinnamon
>
> ½ cup brown sugar
>
> 2 teaspoons gluten-free, dairy-free all-purpose flour
>
> 1 egg, beaten

Glaze

> ¾ cup powdered sugar
>
> ½ teaspoon cinnamon
>
> ¼ teaspoon vanilla extract
>
> 1 tablespoon coconut milk, or alternative milk of your choice

1. Preheat oven to 350°F.

2. Prep 2 baking sheets by covering them with parchment paper and, using a vegetable oil spray, lightly oil the parchment.

3. *Make the tarts:* Separate dough into 2 sections, and roll out on separate parchment paper into 2 separate rectangles. Using a pizza cutter or dough cutter, cut dough into 16 rectangles that will fit together nicely.

4. Combine cinnamon, brown sugar, and flour in a small bowl and set aside.

5. Place a single layer of rectangle dough on each baking sheet. Using a pastry brush, lightly brush each rectangle with beaten egg.

6. Place 2 teaspoons of filling evenly on each rectangle.

7. Cover each rectangle with a matching rectangle of dough and press with your fingers to seal the edges. Using a fork, poke the pastry 4 to 6 times.

8. Using your pastry brush, lightly coat the tops of the tarts with the rest of the beaten egg.

9. Bake for 25 minutes, or until golden brown.

10. Remove from the oven and allow to cool for 15 to 30 minutes.

11. Make the glaze: Sift powdered sugar in a small bowl and add cinnamon, vanilla, and milk. Mix well until completely smooth.

12. Coat each pastry with an equal amount of glaze. Allow to set, then serve.

CRUNCHY CHEESE CRACKERS

G, P, TN, S, E, F, SF (7/8)

So simple and so good, you can eat these alone or add some charcuterie and put more cheese on top! Oh my, do I love cheese. Kids will, too, so make plenty, as they get scarfed down in record time.

Tip: Don't buy the pregrated Parmesan. Instead, I take whole Parmesan and use a Microplane.

PREP TIME: 5 minutes • COOK TIME: 7 minutes • MAKES: 10 servings

4 ounces Parmesan cheese

1. Preheat oven to 400°F. Line a baking sheet with parchment paper and coat lightly with olive oil spray.

2. Grate Parmesan over a bowl using the smallest cheese grater you have.

3. Using a tablespoon, scoop cheese into circles onto baking sheet. Pat down cheese lightly to make a larger circle.

4. Bake for 7 minutes, or until golden brown.

5. Remove from oven and allow to cool before serving.

PRETZEL PUPS

G, D, P, TN, S, F, SF (7/8)

My family has declared this recipe their new favorite on the weekend rotation, and you'll see why when you bake these up yourself. Oh, my, yumness. I like to buy gluten-free pizza dough, or I make the pizza dough recipe from King Arthur Flour gluten-free all-purpose flour for this recipe, and honestly, anytime I'm making a gluten-free pizza. Mostly because you just want to get to the eating part of this recipe quickly. Don't forget to check your condiments for allergens (see Resources on page 197) before you serve these up with delicious sauces.

PREP TIME: 15 minutes • **COOK TIME:** 25 minutes • **MAKES:** 21 servings

¼ cup baking soda

1 ball frozen Wholly Wholesome gluten-free pizza dough, thawed to room temperature

7 hot dogs cut in thirds (I like Applegate for the gluten-free and casein-free element)

1 egg

Sea salt crystals

1. Preheat oven to 425°F. Prepare baking sheet by spraying with vegetable or olive oil spray.

2. Bring 5 cups of water to a boil in a large pot. Add baking soda and allow to dissolve.

3. Meanwhile, roll out pizza dough into a rectangle. Cut strips of pizza dough so they will wrap around hot dog pieces at least twice (approximately 4" to 6"). Place wrapped dogs on baking sheet.

4. Using a strainer or scoop, drop wrapped hot dogs into boiling water 5 or 6 at a time, and allow to boil for 30 seconds before placing them back on baking sheet.

5. Beat egg until frothy, and use a pastry brush to coat each hot dog in egg.

6. Sprinkle sea salt on each dog, and bake for 20 minutes.

7. Serve with mustard, barbecue sauce, ketchup, or whatever your heart desires.

RICE BALLS WITH PEAS

G, P, TN, S, F, SF (6/8)

Risotto is naturally gluten-free and dairy-free, if you skip the cheese (which you can without noticing much of a difference, honestly), but dairy-free breadcrumbs may be difficult to find. While the risotto recipe can be made vegan by using vegetable stock instead of chicken stock, you're going to need that egg to get a good crust on these rice balls. If you're not crazy about crunch and need to be vegan, then try this: roll rice into balls with wet hands, roll in flour, roll in dairy- and egg-free breadcrumbs, then fry.

Kid Tip: Instead of chopping the onion, use a box grater so the onion practically disappears. You won't have any little ones yelling, "What IS that???" Or maybe that's just my kids.

PREP TIME: 30 minutes • **COOK TIME:** 45 minutes • **MAKES:** 20 balls

Risotto

> 4 cups gluten-free chicken or vegetable stock
>
> 3 tablespoons olive oil
>
> 1 onion, grated
>
> 2 cups Arborio rice
>
> ⅓ cup Parmesan cheese, grated
>
> Sea salt
>
> Freshly ground black pepper

Rice Balls

> 2 eggs
>
> 1 cup all-purpose gluten-free, dairy-free flour
>
> 2 cups fine breadcrumbs
>
> 1 cup fresh or frozen peas
>
> ½ cup vegetable oil
>
> Marinara sauce (optional)

1. *Make the risotto:* Heat chicken stock in large saucepan on low, and keep it simmering during entire process.

2. Heat oil on medium-high heat in large Dutch oven and add onions. Cook until softened, approximately 7 minutes.

3. Add rice to Dutch oven and stir to coat with oil and onions. Turn heat down to medium, and cook for 1 to 2 minutes. Adding chicken stock, ½ cup at a time, begin stirring rice continually until rice has soaked up chicken stock. Continue to add chicken stock, ½ cup at a time, stirring until the stock is gone.

4. If rice is still harder than al dente, add water, ¼ cup at a time, until rice is al dente when you bite it.

5. Add Parmesan, salt to taste, and pepper to taste. Remove from heat. Allow risotto to cool either in the refrigerator or at room temperature before making the rice balls.

6. *Make the rice balls:* In a small bowl, beat the eggs until frothy. Set between a plate containing the flour and another plate containing the breadcrumbs.

7. Using your hands, shape risotto into golf ball–size balls. Create a crater in the middle and add 4 or 5 peas. Close up hole and seal.

8. Roll the balls in the flour to completely coat, then in the egg, and then in the breadcrumbs to cover completely. Place on platter or baking sheet, then roll the remaining balls.

9. Heat oil on medium-high heat in a large skillet until water sizzles when you sprinkle it on the oil.

10. Working in batches, fry each ball for 4 to 5 minutes, turning to brown evenly. Remove to paper towel–lined platter to drain.

11. Serve while warm, with a side of marinara sauce, if desired.

CHICKEN TINGA TAQUITOS

G, D, P, TN, S, E, F, SF (8/8)

One of our favorite lunches in our house, the easiest way to make these taquitos is to buy a roasted chicken at the grocery store and get busy. If you're really short on time, find some gluten-free enchilada sauce (see Resources on page 197), warm up the chicken and sauce, and you're good to go. You can serve this up with Mama's Kickin' Black Bean Dip (page 144), Plain Ol' Guacamole (page 141), or both.

PREP TIME: 30 minutes • **COOK TIME:** 40 minutes • **MAKES:** 10 servings

6 tomatoes

1 tablespoon olive oil

2 onions, thinly sliced

1 clove garlic, chopped

½ can (3 ounces) chipotle peppers, in sauce

2 tablespoons gluten-free chicken stock

Whole roasted chicken, shredded

20 corn tortillas

2 cups vegetable oil

1. In a large pot, boil 6 cups of water. Remove stems from tomatoes and add to boiling water. Cook until tomatoes split open, approximately 5 minutes. Drain and set aside.

2. While tomatoes are boiling, heat olive oil over medium-high heat in large skillet. Add onions and cook until transparent. Add garlic and cook for 2 to 3 minutes more. Remove from heat.

3. In a food processor or blender, combine tomatoes, onions, garlic, chipotle peppers (with sauce), and stock, and blend until smooth.

4. Place shredded chicken in the same large skillet used to cook onions and garlic and add processed mixture. Heat on medium and simmer until sauce and chicken are well combined and chicken is heated through. Remove from heat.

5. Warm tortillas, 2 or 3 at a time, by wrapping in a damp paper towel and microwaving for 30 to 45 seconds.

6. Fill tortillas with chicken mixture and roll tightly. Use a toothpick, if necessary, to keep tortillas rolled up tight.

7. Heat vegetable oil on medium-high heat in a deep skillet until surface shimmers. Alternately, if you have a deep-fryer, turn to high.

8. Working in batches, place stuffed tortillas in hot oil and turn once or twice. Cook for 7 to 10 minutes, or until crispy. Remove from oil and drain on paper towel-lined plate.

9. Serve with accoutrements of your choosing.

GO-TO SNACKS THAT ARE NATURALLY SAFE FOR MOST

- All fruit (berries, apples, citrus, mangoes, kiwifruits, grapes, raisins)
- All vegetables (carrot sticks, zucchini zoodles, celery sticks, peas)
- Tasty Brand Organic Fruit Gummy Snacks
- Hippie Butter
- Pumpkin butter (pureed roasted pumpkin for spreading)
- Popcorn (check oils for allergens if not making at home)
- Rice cakes (check additives for allergens)
- Hummus (unless sesame seed–allergic)
- Corn chips (check oils and additives for allergens)
- Potato chips (check oils and additives for allergens)
- Dark chocolate (not milk)
- Luigi's Real Italian Ice
- Enjoy Life Eat Freely snack products (eight main allergen-free)
- Trader Joe's Soft-Baked Snickerdoodles (eight main allergen-free)
- Clif Kid Z Fruit & Veggie Bars

CRÊPE SANDWICHES

G, P, TN, S, F, SF (6/8)

I love an amazing gluten-free crêpe. Or, any crêpe, if I didn't have to eat gluten-free. But, I do! So, I make my entire family and myself very happy by whipping up a batch of gluten-free crêpes every now and then and letting them stuff whatever makes them happy inside. I'm a traditionalist and enjoy good-quality ham and brie, and my kids love turkey and Swiss. Mix and match your sandwich innards in a dozen ways, or add lemon and powdered sugar for a tasty dessert. Honestly, there is no wrong way to eat a crêpe.

PREP TIME: 5 minutes • **COOK TIME:** 7 minutes • **MAKES:** 10 servings

> 7 tablespoons butter
>
> 6 eggs
>
> 3 cups milk
>
> 1 cup all-purpose, gluten-free flour

1. Melt 2 tablespoons butter in a small pan.

2. Mix eggs, milk, and melted butter together in a medium bowl. Slowly whisk in flour until mixture is smooth.

3. Melt ½ tablespoon butter in a lightweight 8-inch skillet or crêpe pan over medium-high heat. Pour ½ cup of batter into the skillet and immediately swirl the pan so the batter coats the entire pan evenly.

4. Cook the crêpe until the edges begin to dry and curl, then flip it over to cook the other side until golden brown, approximately 30 seconds.

5. Remove from pan and transfer to plate. Cover each crêpe with a kitchen towel to keep warm and repeat process, wiping out the pan and melting another ½ tablespoon of butter before adding batter each time.

6. Stuff crêpes with fillings of your choice, roll, and eat.

MUSHROOM QUESADILLAS

G, P, TN, S, E, F, SF (7/8)

When I want to bulk up the regular quesadilla, I sauté some mushrooms and throw them in the mix. It fits easily into a lunch box and travels well. For my avocado-eating child, I add a side of Plain Ol' Guacamole (page 141), but the other one just gets a side of Mama's Kickin' Black Bean Dip (page 144). Make this dish dairy-free and vegan by using Daiya Pepperjack Style Shreds.

PREP TIME: 10 minutes • **COOK TIME:** 15 minutes • **MAKES:** 2 quesadillas

> 4 teaspoons olive oil or butter
> ¼ cup mushrooms, sliced
> Salt and black pepper
> Garlic powder
> 4 corn tortillas (6-inch)
> ½ cup shredded Monterey Jack cheese

1. In a medium skillet, heat 2 teaspoons of oil or butter on medium-high for 1 to 2 minutes.

2. Add mushrooms and sprinkle with salt and pepper, add a dash of garlic powder, and continue to stir while mushrooms soften and darken, approximately 10 minutes. Remove from heat and set aside.

3. Wipe out skillet and add the remaining 2 teaspoons of oil or butter and allow to heat on medium-high again for 1 to 2 minutes.

4. Lay 1 tortilla in skillet, immediately topping with half of the shredded cheese and half of the mushrooms. Lay another tortilla on top and allow to cook for 2 to 3 minutes, or until bottom tortilla starts to brown and get crispy. Flip and cook the other side for the same.

5. Remove quesadilla and repeat with the remaining tortillas. Serve immediately or wrap in foil to transport in your kiddo's lunch box.

BREAKFAST TACOS

G, P, TN, S, F, SF (6/8)

My son loves breakfast tacos any time of day, and I fully appreciate this having grown up in Texas and Oklahoma. A solid breakfast taco starts your day off right, friends. You can either put these in a lunch box, or serve them up the morning after a sleepover. Experiment with the ingredients however you like, but this is the basic bean, cheese, and egg version. Make this dish dairy-free by using Daiya Pepperjack Style Shreds. Traditionally, breakfast tacos are made with flour tortillas; so if you don't have a gluten problem, feel free to use flour. I use corn because, you know, gluten.

PREP TIME: 10 minutes • **COOK TIME:** 10 minutes • **MAKES:** 4 tacos

> 3 eggs
> Butter or olive oil
> 1 cup refried pinto beans
> 4 corn tortillas
> ¼ cup shredded Cheddar or Monterey Jack cheese
> Salsa (optional)

1. In medium bowl, beat eggs until no white appears.

2. Heat skillet on medium-low, add butter or oil, and scramble eggs, stirring frequently. Cook until eggs are desired texture.

3. Heat refried beans in microwave for 60 to 90 seconds, or in a small pot on medium-high heat.

4. Heat tortillas in skillet over low heat individually, or place tortillas covered with a wet paper towel in a microwave for 20 to 30 seconds.

5. Make tacos by placing an even amount of eggs, beans, and cheese in each tortilla and roll.

6. Serve with a side of salsa, if desired.

MINI FROZEN FRUIT KABOBS

G, D, P, TN, S, E, F, SF (8/8)

I like these snacks for lunch boxes, because they'll still be a little bit chilled by lunchtime, or to serve up at a playdate. They're simple, allergy-friendly, and fun. We prefer to use grapes or to cut up plums into smaller pieces, but you can use any fruit that freezes well.

Tip: Berries don't freeze as well as stone fruits and grapes. Mango is also great.

PREP TIME: 5 minutes • **CHILL TIME:** 1 hour • **MAKES:** 5 kabobs

2 cups fresh fruit, cut into grape-size pieces

1. Skewer fruit pieces onto kabob sticks. Allow to freeze for at least an hour, but you can leave in longer and have kabobs all week.

2. Remove from freezer and eat immediately, or pop into your kiddo's lunch box in a waterproof container.

CHICKEN SATAY

D, P, TN, E (4/8)

PREP TIME: 15 minutes • **CHILL TIME:** 3 hours • **COOK TIME:** 10 minutes • **MAKES:** 4 servings

4 chicken breasts or 2 pounds chicken tenders

2 tablespoons SunButter

1 tablespoon coconut cream

Juice of 4 limes

2 tablespoons wheat-free tamari or soy sauce

1 tablespoon sugar

2 teaspoons Annie's Vegan Worchestershire Sauce (or fish sauce, which would make this dish gluten-free)

1 tablespoon curry powder

1 teaspoon Sriracha

½ white onion, thinly sliced

2 cloves garlic, quartered

Shredded cabbage, cilantro, and lime wedges (optional)

1. Pound chicken breasts to ½" thick. Cut into 1" to 2" strips and set aside.

2. Whisk together SunButter, coconut cream, lime juice, tamari or soy sauce, sugar, fish sauce, curry powder, and Sriracha until well mixed. Pour mixture into gallon-size zip-top bag and add onion and garlic.

3. Place chicken inside zip-top bag and make sure all is covered well. Allow to marinate in the refrigerator for at least 3 hours, or overnight.

4. Heat grill on high for 15 minutes, and soak 12 bamboo skewers in water.

5. Thread chicken onto skewers. Place skewers evenly spaced on grill. Cook for 3 to 5 minutes per side, until slightly crispy. Cut open to make sure chicken is cooked through, and remove from grill.

6. Serve with shredded cabbage, cilantro, and lime, if desired.

MONSTER COOKIES

G, P, TN, F, SF (5/8)

PREP TIME: 15 minutes • **COOK TIME:** 12 minutes • **MAKES:** 4 dozen cookies

2 sticks butter, softened

1 cup granulated sugar

1 cup packed brown sugar

3 large eggs

½ teaspoon vanilla extract

½ teaspoon corn syrup

2 teaspoons baking soda

1½ cups SunButter

4½ cups gluten-free rolled oats

2 cups semi-sweet chocolate chips

2 cups plain M&Ms

1. Preheat oven to 350°F.

2. In a large bowl, cream the butter, sugar, and brown sugar. Add the eggs, one at a time, and mix between each addition. Add the vanilla, corn syrup, baking soda, and SunButter. Mix well until smooth.

3. Add the oats and mix well, scraping the sides of the bowl. Add the chocolate chips and mix until they are evenly distributed throughout the batter. Then add the M&Ms and mix well.

4. Using about a tablespoon of batter for each, roll the batter into balls and place them 2" apart on ungreased baking sheets.

5. Bake until the edges are golden brown, 10 to 12 minutes.

6. Let cool on baking sheets for about 2 minutes before transferring to cooling racks. Cookies will stay fresh for up to 5 days in a sealed container.

SUNBUTTER SUNDAES

G, P, TN, S, E, F, SF (7/8)

PREP TIME: 10 minutes • **COOK TIME:** 8 minutes • **MAKES:** 6 servings

1 cup sugar
½ cup SunButter
Ice cream
Hot fudge sauce, whipped cream, and cherries (optional)

1. In a medium saucepan, dissolve sugar in ½ cup water and bring mixture to a boil. Add SunButter and mix completely.

2. Assemble sundaes by scooping ice cream into a bowl, adding hot fudge, if desired, and pouring SunButter sauce on top. Add whipped cream, cherries, or other toppings, if desired.

SUNBUTTER CRISPY TREATS

P, TN, S, E, F, SF (6/8)

PREP TIME: 10 minutes • **COOK TIME:** 10 minutes • **MAKES:** 12 servings

3 tablespoons butter, plus more for smoothing
4 cups marshmallows
½ cup SunButter
6 cups puffed rice cereal

1. In a large saucepan, melt butter and marshmallows over medium-high heat. Stir until completely smooth. Add SunButter and mix completely.

2. Remove from heat, add puffed rice cereal, and quickly combine completely.

3. Transfer to a parchment paper-covered baking sheet and press mixture evenly by using a buttered spatula or your hands.

4. Allow treats to cool, and cut into squares to serve.

SUNBUTTER FUDGE

G, P, TN, S, E, F, SF (7/8)

PREP TIME: 15 minutes • **COOK TIME:** 15 minutes • **MAKES:** 15 servings

2 cups sugar
½ cup half-and-half
1 cup SunButter
4 ounces dark chocolate

1. Prepare a 9-inch square baking pan by spraying vegetable oil spray on surface and covering with parchment paper.

2. In a medium saucepan, dissolve sugar in half-and-half over medium-high heat, bringing it to a boil. Add SunButter and mix completely until smooth. Remove from heat and pour into prepared pan.

3. While fudge is firming up, melt chocolate in a microwave for 30 seconds at a time until smooth.

4. Using a knife or other instrument, swirl chocolate over the fudge evenly. Allow the mixture to cool, then cut into squares to serve.

Chapter

7

How to Make Bake Sales
Your B*tch

Listen up, haters, this chapter is for you. It's totally cool that you pack your kid's lunch with whatever the hell he'll eat (except peanut butter, right??????), and that you never learn how to make a gluten- and dairy-free hot dog bun. It truly is. We parents have enough on our plate without complicating the morning routine by making every lunch into a vegan paradise. (Unless you are a vegan, obvs.) But now, we're going to talk about serving others, and this is where so many of us get stopped and throw up our hands as if to say, "¯_(ツ)_/¯." It's hard enough to prepare food for your own family with all of their "I can't eat anything with green stuff on it" and "Oh, I didn't tell you? I'm a 'porkaterian' now" bullshit. Add in a few other kids to the mix, and it's downright terrifying. So, it makes sense to just forget about this whole baking for others thing and move on. I get it.

If you're like me, you mostly ignore any and all e-mails that come from your child's school for this reason, and many other good ones. You can only read about the latest pinkeye breakout so many times before you embrace the philosophy of, "Let Go and Let God." And this is how I have mostly avoided providing baked goods for 5-plus years of elementary school events!

Apparently, God doesn't want me baking for kindergarteners. Understood.

But I did reconsider my no-baking policy once I learned about a newly diagnosed celiac in our community. I realized that if I didn't provide some gluten-free chocolate chip cookies, no one would. Except for his parents, of course, but they were probably too busy freaking out about letting their little dude eat in public, much less trying to find a great gluten-free, nut-free, kosher recipe for shortbread. As I began to hear about more and more kids with food allergies and intolerances, I knew that a bake sale without options would be a very sad bake sale, indeed. All of a sudden, I wasn't the only one walking by the rows of bento box–shaped cookies and luscious pieces of chocolate cake, crying because I would never know the feel of a pecan tart pie crust crunching all around my mouth ever again. The exclusive bake sale treats were no longer only upsetting to me—an adult who, in theory, can tolerate the pain of flaky pastry denial. I knew at that point that I must think about the children. THE CHILDREN!!!! Of course, I also wanted to eat a lemon bar that wouldn't make me poop my pants, but if I lost control of my bowels, at least it wouldn't be in front of a group of 8-year-old boys during gym class. Probably. From that point on, I vowed to re-create allergy-friendly treats to offer up whenever I was called upon to do so. This, my friends, is easier said than done. That doesn't mean that you shouldn't do it, though.

Go Big or Go Home: Freedom Isn't Free

You may wonder why I'm throwing out all of the big guns of slogans right now. It's because it's so incredibly important to make food safely for kids with allergies. In a totally disgusting way to illustrate this point, I'm actually writing this in between racing to the toilet to destroy the sanctity of my bathroom. You see, I just got back from a school bake sale where I enjoyed a gluten-free cookie (or three) made by a well-meaning(?) parent. Totally had gluten in it, and now I'm missing a much-needed sushi night with my lady friends due to the fact that I cannot be out of the bathroom for more than 5-minute increments. I know that you're not really feeling me, you people out there who know sushi is for coastal snobs and catfish bait, but stay with me for a minute.

You're probably wondering how in the world to be mindful of the kids who can't eat everything, while also not embarrassing yourself with some dried-out quinoa cookies wrapped up in shimmery blue cellophane. Hey, at least the wrapping looks good! The fact is that the most allergy-friendly treats for masses of children are going to be the ones with simple ingredients that are naturally allergy-free. I'm talking fruits, vegetables, limited nonoffending grains such as rice, and if you aren't vegan—meat. Mmmm, meat treat. Keep it naturally safe, and you'll have a load of easy recipes to trot out and zero headaches about any complicated substitutions that may or may not be safe for every single kid in attendance. For example, some gluten-free flours contain dairy (see "Gluten Substitutes" on page 108), and some butter substitutes contain soy (see "Butter Substitutes" on page 107). Not to mention that, once you start removing things like gluten and dairy, sometimes you need to add sugar. Mmmm, delicious sugar. But not so awesome if you're filling up your allergic kids with sugar in lieu of other things all the time. Sometimes? Special occasions? You bet. But not every day, because you'll have a host of other problems on your hands. Still, there's a reason I have recipes for cakes, pies, and hot dog buns, and that reason is that I want to eat those things. And so do kids!

This is why we're here, right? We want cake, and we don't want it to harm anyone. So let's dig into these baked-good recipes that you can enjoy at home when your daughter's allergic BFF comes over, or you can make in bulk and take to the bake sale with confidence. Some recipes will cover all of the eight allergens, some will cover most, but you can mix and match your allergens with help from my handy-dandy substitutions list below, where I help you make a dairy-filled cake dairy-free and teach you how to fake eggs (among other tricks of the allergic trade) and understand why sometimes it's go egg or go home (I'm looking at you, lemon bars). These special treats will be what you trot out for birthday parties and classroom celebrations from now on, because YUM.

How to Not Screw Up

There are many ways to screw up in the kitchen, and, believe me, I've done most of them. We're still trying to get that chocolate-barbecue sauce off my kitchen ceiling. It becomes very crucial to avoid screwing up, however, when you're handling food for kids who could react badly to an allergen. Crucial. While you're preparing these allergy-free recipes, please keep the following in mind.

Wrap It for Safety

You must prepare allergy-free food on clean surfaces and in clean pots, pans, and baking sheets. You absolutely cannot boil some gluten-free pasta for your mac and cheese in the same pot you just used to boil up your gluten-filled pasta. You cannot bake an egg- and dairy-free cookie on a sheet that has been habitually used to bake cookies chock-full of eggs and dairy without covering it with parchment or scrubbing it so hard you probably scrub off the nonstick surface. You can scrub pots and pans within an inch of their lives, but if they have even a crumb of allergen left over, it's possible it will stick on your nice, allergy-free dough. You also cannot bake nut-filled cookies on the same sheet as their nutless brothers and sisters. This may sound like a pain, so I have two words that will make it much easier to keep things clean and separate: *aluminum foil*. Oh, and two more: *parchment paper*.

Before you bake, cover your bakeware with aluminum foil, or parchment paper for the cookies that stick. Before you grill, place aluminum foil down on the grill that will hold your allergy-free options. If you don't have a cutting board, or very clean surface to prepare your safe food, put down aluminum foil or parchment paper. Your new best friend is aluminum foil. Get to know him, along with his BFF, parchment paper.

No Holding Hands or PDA

When you're preparing food, keep the allergens far away from the allergen-free ingredients. If they get mixed up, your allergen-free dish is toast. Don't use the same cutting board for fish that you do for chicken, if you have a fish-allergic guest. Also, don't think fish is a great ingredient for a school bake sale or a 6-year-old birthday party. That's a mistake you'll only make once.

Additionally, don't let all this hard work keeping surfaces bleached and ingredients separate go to waste by serving up all of your safe food on a platter alongside the dangerous food. Continue to keep these foods separate, using separate cooking pots, pans, and sheets, as well as separate utensils. Consciously uncouple the allergy-laden from the allergy-free foods to make sure that the end result is safe for all.

Whew! That's a lot, but if you remember to keep your allergy-safe treats safe from the first time you pick up the ingredients until they are safely delivered to the sale, you'll make a heck of a lot of kiddos happy, as well as their very anxious parents. It's like farm to table, but without the hipster element.

A much more exhaustive list of allergy-friendly products lives in the resource section of this book (see page 197), but if you want to get started baking right away, here are a few items to consider stocking in your pantry before you put on your allergen-free apron. (Okay, that's not a real thing, so don't panic. Any old apron without clumps of food on it will do.)

Butter Substitutes

Earth Balance—This vegan butter alternative comes in many forms, but you'll most likely be picking up the baking sticks for the following recipes. If you're making a soy-free treat, do not buy the buttery baking sticks, but instead pick up the soy-free version.

Nutiva Organic Vegan Superfood Shortening—This soy-free, dairy-free, gluten-free, GMO (genetically modified organism)-free, fair-trade product is a combination of red palm oil and virgin coconut oil. You can find a million different coconut oils on the market, but Nutiva's combination with palm oil makes it a better option for baking when you're avoiding the eight main allergens.

Crisco Vegetable Shortening, Butter Flavor—I grew up using Crisco butter flavor in so many family recipes that I naturally tried it first when I went about experimenting with dairy-free baked goods. While my family probably used Crisco as a butter substitute for completely different, now-defunct reasons (it was the 1980s, and butter was the enemy), it does hold up in recipes pretty well. Crisco contains soy, along with artificial flavors, so if you're not on board with either of those, you should probably try Spectrum organic all-vegetable shortening. The main ingredient in both vegetable shortening brands is also palm oil.

Egg Substitutes

Ener-G Egg Replacer—The OG of egg replacement, Ener-G has been helping out egg-free bakers for a very long time. If you're going to be baking egg-free a lot, I would suggest grabbing a box and going to town. Since it's also eight main allergen-free, it's a good substitute for the kids.

Golden Flax Meal—Flax meal has become my go-to for baking without eggs. You combine 1 tablespoon of flax meal with 3 tablespoons of water per egg called for in the recipe. The key is in letting it sit for a little while before you use it. (I say at least 10 minutes, but if you have a half-hour to wait, do that for optimum egglike properties.) You can either buy the golden flaxseeds and grind them in a coffee grinder when you're ready to use them, or buy the meal and keep it sealed up tight so it will retain its freshness.

Chia Seeds—Chia seeds work in the same manner as flaxseeds, and are truly gelatinous. My only issue is if you're creating something light in color, you can get a little black spot action in the final product. Both work well, so go with what you like.

Follow Your Heart VeganEgg—What's great about this all-allergen-free product is that you can even cook this up and make an omelet if you've been craving one since you had to go egg-free.

Baking Soda and Vinegar—I've used the baking-soda-and-vinegar combo in a pinch and, while it didn't seem to work as well as the magic flax meal, it's definitely serviceable in your baked goods. Combine 1 teaspoon of baking soda and 1 tablespoon of vinegar (watch, as it will bubble up), allow to dissolve, and you have a substitute for 1 egg.

Gluten Substitutes

Cup4Cup—For baking, I've always loved Cup4Cup multi-purpose gluten-free flour, but it will not work as a flour in the dairy-free recipes, as one of the ingredients is milk powder. I also like to use all-purpose flours so

I don't have to experiment with xanthan gum or add anything else to the mix. It makes it easier, and that makes me happier.

Better Batter—Luckily, my other favorite gluten-free, all-purpose flour is dairy-free (and every other allergen-free, plus kosher), and it also gives fantastic results. It's become one of my go-tos now that I'm experimenting with gluten- and dairy-free recipes, but it is sadly harder to find than many other popular brands. I recommend ordering online and stocking up if you're going to be the bake-sale queen.

King Arthur Gluten-Free All-Purpose—Another great gluten- and dairy-free option, I also love to use King Arthur's recipes. It's a solid choice, and I almost always have a box in my cupboard.

Almond Meal—Only if you know there are no nut allergies around, almond meal makes for some delicious cakes. The texture is lovely and moist, and the slight nutty flavor can enhance any cake recipe. You do have to experiment with it, unlike the all-purpose flours above, but if you're 100 percent sure that you don't need to keep it tree-nut-free, have some fun with the almond flour family.

Milk Substitutes

The trouble with milk substitutes in baking is the lack of eight main allergen-free options if (and this is a pretty big if) you have a coconut problem. While rice milk fits the bill, it is not as rich and appropriate for baking as coconut milk cream and coconut milk are. Soy milk and nut milks are also great substitutes, but have the obvious problem of being in the eight main allergen family.

I generally recommend coconut cream and coconut milk regardless, as a coconut allergy as part of a tree-nut allergy is so incredibly rare. And when it comes to baked goods, coconut milk does have the best result in a recipe. Still, be sure you know the specifics of any allergies kids may have before you start to mix up your eight main allergen-free brownies.

One more note for the bake-sale bakers, before we dive into recipes: If you're preparing food for a party, bake sale, or anywhere that you will be dropping off and not sticking around to explain what's up with your cookies, label your treats. Let the dairy-free know if something is safe to eat by being very clear with your packaging. After all, what's the point of making allergy-friendly treats if no one knows about it? (Note to parents of the severely allergic: You still don't want to risk homemade treats from someone's kitchen unless you've had a very detailed convo and know without a doubt that they're safe for your kiddo. But you knew that already, I'm sure.)

Now, stock up on your cellophane and decorative twine . . . it's bake sale time!

Key

Gluten (G), Dairy (D), Peanuts (P), Tree Nuts (TN),
Soy (S), Egg (E), Fish (F), and Shellfish (SF)—
means it is free of these allergens.

HOT COCOA CUBES

G, P, TN, S, E, F, SF (7/8)

This is one of the easiest treats to make for a bake sale, or for holiday gifts, and my kids and I have started a tradition of making Hot Cocoa Cubes for all! Seriously, it's that easy. While you can keep it dairy-free by only using dark chocolate, if you don't have an issue, pick whatever chocolate you like, even white. I do think it tastes much better when it's melted into milk, rather than water, so the dairy may become a moot point. Of course, there is always the warmed-up milk alternative for those who cannot deal with the dairy.

PREP TIME: 10 minutes • **COOK TIME:** 10 minutes • **CHILL TIME:** 1 hour
MAKES: 10 large or 16 small cubes

> 16 ounces gluten-free, dairy-free high-quality chocolate (see Resources on page 197)
>
> ⅓ cup gluten-free, dairy-free cocoa powder
>
> 1 cup powdered sugar, sifted
>
> Toppings (check packages for allergens): crushed candy canes, exotic sea salts, marshmallows, caramel sauce, and rock candy

1. Prepare 1 or 2 silicon ice trays (depending on size), making sure the inside is completely dry.

2. Chop the chocolate into 1" pieces and place in a medium microwave-safe bowl. Microwave in 30-second increments until chocolate is smooth and melted.

3. Remove chocolate from microwave and mix in cocoa and powdered sugar until completely smooth.

4. Using a pastry bag with a tip, or a zip-top bag with a corner cut off, fill bag with mixture. Pipe chocolate mixture into ice trays evenly and sprinkle toppings of your choice on top of each cube.

5. Insert ice pop sticks or small plastic spoons (not normal size) into center of each cube.

6. Place trays in refrigerator for an hour until they are firm.

7. Remove from trays and wrap individually.

CREME-FILLED SPONGE CAKES

G, D, P, TN, F, SF (6/8)

No one is going to take away my Twinkies. Well, okay, they have been taken away, but that doesn't mean I can't try and re-create these bad boys in my own kitchen, and at least impress the bake-sale committee with this old-school treat, which is now allergy-friendly. Let's talk about all the options that will make these little cakes allergy-free. If you use marshmallow creme, you will be using a product that has eggs and is not vegan. If you use Ricemellow creme in the filling, it's vegan, but has soy. SO, if you have a soy allergy to contend with, but are safe with eggs, go for marshmallow creme. Need it vegan and can have soy, go Ricemellow. Yep, this is one of those recipes that has so much going on that it's much easier to make it dairy- and gluten-free than free of any other allergen in town. It may seem way too complicated, but just wait until you see what issues come up in the next recipe.

While you can use a hot dog bun mold (and yes, they do even have Twinkie molds), if you don't want to invest in that kind of kitchen action, you can make molds out of aluminum foil. You take a 10" piece of aluminum foil (didn't I tell you it would be your BFF?), and fold it into threes. Use a medium spice jar to help guide you as you fold the sides up and over to create a Twinkie-size boat.

PREP TIME: 20 minutes • **COOK TIME:** 40 minutes • **MAKES:** 12 cakes

Cakes

1½ cups all-purpose gluten-free, dairy-free flour

1 cup granulated sugar

1 teaspoon baking powder

1 teaspoon baking soda

⅓ cup vegetable oil

1 teaspoon vanilla extract

1 tablespoon apple-cider vinegar

Filling

½ cup vegetable shortening

7 ounces marshmallow or Ricemellow creme

¼ teaspoon salt

⅓ cup powdered sugar

2 tablespoons hot water

½ teaspoon vanilla extract

1. Preheat oven to 350°F. Make 12 aluminum foil boats and place on a baking sheet, or use a mold. Spray molds liberally with vegetable oil baking spray (gluten-free) and set aside.

2. *Make the cakes:* In a large bowl, whisk together flour, sugar, baking powder, and baking soda.

3. In a smaller bowl, whisk together oil, 1 cup water, vanilla, and vinegar. Make a well in the middle of the dry ingredients and add wet ingredients and mix well.

4. Pour batter into molds in equal parts, and bake for 35 minutes, or until golden brown. You may need to place them under the broiler for 1 to 2 minutes to get the edges crispy and brown.

5. Remove from oven and allow to cool completely.

6. *Make the filling:* Combine shortening and marshmallow or Ricemellow creme thoroughly. Then add salt, powdered sugar, water, and vanilla. Mix until completely smooth and pour filling into a pastry bag with straight tip or into a zip-top bag with a corner cut off to create a piping tool.

7. Using a straw, poke 3 holes in the cake down the center. Fill each sponge cake with filling. Enjoy the heck out of them.

CREME-FILLED CHOCOLATE CUPCAKES

G, D, P, F, SF (5/8)

Not to be left out, the cupcakes of our packaged youth can also be made allergy-friendly. A few tips from my experimenting: Don't try the zip-top bag piping tool, as you need a strong tip and an easy way to fill up those cakes. Plastic sandwich bags won't cut it here. I've found that coconut milk makes for the best dairy-free ganache, but if you have a tree-nut allergy that you're working around, try soy milk. If you must go egg-free and vegan, go for the Ricemellow creme, as the marshmallow creme is not vegan. If you have a soy problem, you cannot use the Ricemellow creme. Finally, if you're showing off at the bake sale, may I suggest you do the icing loops on top? (Not as easy, nor required, for those of us with zero crafty talent.)

PREP TIME: 25 minutes • **COOK TIME:** 35 minutes • **CHILL TIME:** 20 minutes
MAKES: 12 cupcakes

Cupcakes

- 1½ cups all-purpose gluten-free, dairy-free flour
- 1 cup granulated sugar
- 3 tablespoons cocoa powder
- 1 teaspoon baking soda
- ½ teaspoon salt
- 1 teaspoon apple-cider vinegar
- 1 teaspoon vanilla extract
- 5 tablespoons vegetable oil

Filling

- ¼ teaspoon salt
- 2 tablespoons hot water
- 7 ounces marshmallow or Ricemellow creme
- ½ cup vegetable shortening
- ⅓ cup powdered sugar
- ½ teaspoon vanilla extract

Ganache

- ¾ cup coconut milk (or soy milk if there is a tree-nut allergy that includes coconut)
- 1 cup nondairy dark chocolate chunks

1. Preheat oven to 350°F and line 2 muffin pans with paper cupcake liners.

2. *Make the cupcakes:* In a large bowl, whisk together flour, sugar, cocoa powder, baking soda, and salt.

3. In a medium bowl, mix vinegar, vanilla, oil, and 1 cup water.

4. Create a well in the dry ingredients and pour in wet ingredients and combine.

5. Bake for 35 minutes or until toothpick comes out clean in center of test cupcake.

6. Allow cupcakes to cool for 10 minutes.

7. *Make the filling:* In a small bowl, dissolve salt in hot water. Set aside.

8. Using a hand mixer or stand mixer, combine marshmallow or Ricemellow creme, shortening, powdered sugar, and vanilla until completely smooth.

9. Once cupcakes have cooled, remove paper from cupcakes and set on a tray. Using a pastry bag with tip, fill each cupcake with cream by poking a hole in the bottom and squeezing until you can feel the cupcake give a little bit. Set cupcakes back on tray.

10. Make the ganache: In a medium pot, bring coconut milk to light boil. Add chocolate and stir regularly until completely combined. Remove ganache from heat and allow to cool for 10 minutes or until it is cool enough to dip cupcakes.

11. Dip the tops of each cupcake into the ganache, and return to tray. Place tray in refrigerator for 20 minutes. Remove from the fridge and pipe on a little loop pattern, using some allergy-friendly white icing, and serve.

CARAMEL APPLES

G, P, TN, S, E, F, SF (7/8)

I grew up with those caramel wraps you stuck over an apple and microwaved, and, wow, was that fun. Unfortunately, for the allergic, those wraps are filled with soy, tree nuts, and possibly gluten, so they're not exactly allergy-friendly. It's actually incredibly easy to make your own caramel, and to just dip those apples like mad. Roll those goodies in some other special treats, and you have a party on your hands. Or, at least a pretty dang good bake-sale item.

PREP TIME: 20 minutes • **COOK TIME:** 45 minutes • **CHILL TIME:** 30 minutes
MAKES: 10 apples

> 2 cups granulated sugar
>
> 1 cup brown sugar
>
> 1 cup corn syrup
>
> 1 cup evaporated milk
>
> 1 pint heavy whipping cream
>
> 1 cup butter
>
> 2 teaspoons vanilla extract
>
> 10 apples
>
> Toppings: colored sugar, pretzel bits (gluten-free options), and chocolate chips

1. In a large Dutch oven on medium-high heat, combine sugar, brown sugar, corn syrup, evaporated milk, whipping cream, and butter. Cook on medium heat, stirring regularly.

2. Once mixture reaches 240°F (hard-ball stage), remove mixture from heat and add vanilla. Continue stirring to cool mixture for 10 minutes. You don't want the caramel to be so hot that it affects the apple texture.

3. Once the caramel mixture has cooled and thickened, you're ready to dunk the apples. Remove stems from apples, and place an ice pop stick into the tops, pushing in halfway.

4. Using a ladle or fork to help guide you, dunk each apple into caramel mixture, roll in toppings, and place on parchment paper-lined baking sheets.

5. Place apples in refrigerator for 30 minutes to help set quickly. Store in a cool, dry place.

LEMON BARS

G, D, P, TN, S, F, SF (7/8)

Everyone loves a lemon bar, but not everyone loves dairy. Substitute Earth Balance in your favorite recipe, or try this butter-flavored shortening version. As always, if you don't have to be gluten-free, use a cup-for-cup all-purpose flour instead of my favorite all-purpose gluten-free, dairy-free flour.

PREP TIME: 15 minutes • **COOK TIME:** 55 minutes • **MAKES:** 25 bars

Crust

> ½ cup Spectrum butter-flavored vegetable shortening
>
> ¼ cup powdered sugar
>
> 1 cup granulated sugar
>
> 1 cup all-purpose gluten-free, dairy-free flour

Filling

> 6 eggs, room temperature
>
> 1 tablespoon lemon zest
>
> 1 cup lemon juice
>
> 3 cups granulated sugar
>
> 1 cup all-purpose gluten-free, dairy-free flour

Topping

> ¼ cup powdered sugar

1. Preheat oven to 350°F.

2. *Make the crust:* Combine shortening, powdered sugar, and granulated sugar with an electric mixer until creamy. Scrape sides and stir in flour. Combine well. Mixture will be slightly crumbly.

3. Transfer dough to a parchment paper-covered, oiled 9" square pan, and press around edges to make crust even.

4. Bake for 20 minutes, or until brown.

5. *Make the filling:* Beat eggs in a medium bowl. Stir in lemon zest, lemon juice, and sugar. Sprinkle in flour, and combine until smooth.

6. Pour over crust and bake for 35 minutes, or until center firms up.

7. Allow to cool, then sift powdered sugar on top.

IT'S A TRUFFLE PARTY!

G, D, P, TN, S, E, F, SF (8/8)

Easy to make and easy to eat in one sitting, truffles are a hit for bake sales, holidays, after-dinner treats . . . you get the idea. Truffles rule! Make some today.

PREP TIME: 10 minutes • **COOK TIME:** 5 minutes • **CHILL TIME:** 3 hours • **MAKES:** 15 truffles

> 10 ounces gluten-free, dairy-free chocolate (see Resources on page 197)
>
> ½ cup coconut milk
>
> ¼ teaspoon vanilla extract
>
> Toppings: dairy-free cocoa powder, colored sugar crystals, powdered sugar, and sweetened coconut flakes

1. Chop chocolate into chunks and place in a medium bowl.

2. Using a double-boiler, bring coconut milk to medium boil. Remove coconut milk from heat and pour over chocolate chunks. Begin mixing immediately. Add vanilla and mix well.

3. After chocolate mixture is completely smooth, cover and place in refrigerator to chill for 3 hours.

4. Once chocolate is scoopable, using a tablespoon, roll chocolate into balls and place on a platter.

5. Choose your toppings, and roll truffles until covered completely. Return to refrigerator until ready to serve.

COCONUT KEY LIME MOUSSE

G, D, P, TN, S, F, SF (7/8)

This delicious summer treat is so refreshing, and will make you think you're on vacation. Maybe just for a little bit, anyway. I would highly recommend buying a bottle of key lime juice presqueezed, as squeezing those little bitty limes is a pain in the butt. Of course, you could employ your children for that job, and then you can sit back and enjoy the results. Package these in little aluminum foil tins and you have a bake-sale option.

PREP TIME: 15 minutes • **COOK TIME:** 10 minutes • **CHILL TIME:** 1 hour • **MAKES:** 10 servings

Filling

> 3 egg yolks
>
> ½ cup granulated sugar
>
> ⅔ cup key lime juice (from approximately 1 pound key limes)
>
> Zest of 2 key limes
>
> 14 ounces coconut milk
>
> 1 tablespoon all-purpose gluten-free, dairy-free flour

Coconut Whipped Cream

> 1½ cups coconut cream
>
> ¼ cup powdered sugar
>
> Lime zest, for garnish (optional)

1. *Make the filling:* Whisk together egg yolks, sugar, lime juice, lime zest, and coconut milk in a large saucepan. Whisk in flour.

2. Place pan on medium-high heat and stir continuously until mixture has thickened to a custard texture, approximately 10 minutes. Remove from heat.

3. Fill 10 small ramekins or bowls with mixture and transfer to refrigerator for 1 hour.

4. *Make the coconut whipped cream:* Combine coconut cream and powdered sugar in a medium bowl. Beat mixture on high until light and fluffy.

5. Remove mousse from refrigerator and serve with a dollop of whipped cream. Add lime zest, if desired.

CUPCAKE BOWLS WITH FRUIT FILLING

G, D, P, TN, S, E, F, SF (8/8)

A festive-looking and allergy-friendly dessert, cupcake bowls are also an incredibly easy treat to make for a crowd. Heck, I even employ the kids when I'm making cupcake bowls, because I know that they'll enthusiastically dig into the cupcake tops, because they want to eat the pieces that "fall off" during the process. I prefer to fill these up with mixed berries and a sprig of mint with a drizzle of chocolate sauce on top, or a crumble of the leftover cupcake tops. But you do you.

PREP TIME: 15 minutes • **COOK TIME:** 30 minutes • **MAKES:** 24 cupcakes

Cupcakes

1½ cups all-purpose gluten-free, dairy-free flour

1 cup sugar

3 tablespoons cocoa powder

1 teaspoon baking soda

½ teaspoon salt

1 teaspoon apple-cider vinegar

1 teaspoon vanilla extract

5 tablespoons vegetable oil

Filling

3 cups mixed fresh berries

½ cup sugar

Chocolate sauce and mint sprigs (optional)

1. Preheat oven to 350°F and line 2 muffin pans with paper cupcake liners.

2. *Make the cupcakes:* In a large bowl, whisk together flour, sugar, cocoa powder, baking soda, and salt. Set aside.

3. In a medium bowl, mix together vinegar, vanilla, oil, and 1 cup water.

4. Create a well in the dry ingredients and pour in wet ingredients, and combine. Pour batter into muffin pans.

5. Bake for 30 minutes, or until toothpick comes out clean from center of test cupcake.

6. Remove from oven and allow to cool for 15 minutes.

7. *Make the filling:* In a medium saucepan, combine berries, sugar, and ¼ cup water, and mix well. Bring mixture to a boil and allow it to boil for 5 minutes, stirring regularly. Remove from heat and set aside to cool.

8. Remove cupcakes from liners and line up on a serving platter.

9. Using a small ice cream scoop or large spoon, scoop out the center of the cupcakes and set aside the crumbs.

10. Evenly distribute the berry mixture inside each "bowl."

11. Drizzle with chocolate sauce and add a sprig of mint, if desired, or crumble leftover cupcake crumbs on top and serve.

Fun Tip: Fill these up with ice cream of your choice (see Resources on page 197) and add fruit on top with chocolate syrup for cupcake sundaes at your next birthday party.

NUT-FREE CARROT CAKE

G, P, TN, S, F, SF (6/8)

My mother, God bless her, used to make a number of nut-free desserts, thanks to a very picky daughter. Yes, it was I. And yes, I do love all manner of nut toppings as an adult. So I grew up enjoying nut-free fudge and this, a nut-free carrot cake, even though it's better with pecans, walnuts, and whatever else you want to throw in there. But this means I'm totally clear on how to make it safe for the nut-allergy crew. Hooray! Still, that cream cheese frosting is not going to work with your dairy-free crowd. Honestly, you could bake this as a sheet cake (add 10 minutes to baking time) and powder sugar the top within an inch of its life. Sub in that Earth Balance, and you're good to go dairy-free.

PREP TIME: 1 hour • **COOK TIME:** 30 minutes • **CHILL TIME:** 1 hour • **MAKES:** 12 servings

Cake

- 3 eggs
- 1 cup vegetable oil, plus more for greasing pans
- 1½ cups granulated sugar
- 2 cups all-purpose gluten-free, dairy-free flour, plus more for dusting
- 2 teaspoons cinnamon
- 1 teaspoon baking soda
- 1 teaspoon vanilla extract
- ½ teaspoon salt
- 3 cups shredded carrots (5 medium)

Cream Cheese Frosting

- 8 ounces cream cheese, softened
- ½ stick butter
- 4 cups powdered sugar, sifted
- 1 teaspoon vanilla extract

1. Preheat oven to 350°F.

2. Grease and flour two 9-inch round pans, and set aside.

3. *Make the cake:* Using a stand or hand mixer, beat eggs until frothy. Add oil and sugar, and combine well.

4. Mix in flour, cinnamon, baking soda, vanilla, and salt. Gently fold in carrots, and allow mixture to stand for 5 minutes.

5. Transfer mixture evenly into 2 round pans and bake for 30 minutes, or until toothpick comes out clean from the center. Allow cakes to cool for at least an hour.

6. *Make the cream cheese frosting:* In a stand mixer, or using a hand mixer, beat cream cheese and butter until smooth. Add sugar and mix well. Add vanilla and beat for 1 to 2 minutes until completely smooth.

7. Spread a small amount of frosting on cake tops and sides, and allow to dry for 30 minutes or more. Using the remaining frosting, frost and assemble the cake, finishing by smoothing the outer icing.

SUNBUTTER BUCKEYES

G, P, TN, E, F, SF (6/8)

Traditional buckeyes are a delicious combo of chocolate and peanut butter. I've made these nuggets of love for many different crowds, substituting almond butter and now, SunButter, to make it friendly for the proper crowd. My panel of taste-testers (ahem, people I'm related to) swear that they love each one equally, which is quite a feat. I'd suggest that you tailor these buckeyes to the allergy you're dealing with at the moment, or if you're not sure about the crowd, go with the least-allergic element of the bunch—SunButter.

PREP TIME: 30 minutes • **COOK TIME:** 10 minutes • **CHILL TIME:** 1 hour • **MAKES:** 24 buckeyes

> 1 cup SunButter
>
> 2 tablespoons softened butter
>
> ½ cup powdered sugar, plus more if needed
>
> ¾ cup brown sugar
>
> 12 ounces semi-sweet chocolate chips

1. Line a baking sheet with wax paper and set aside.

2. In the bowl of a stand mixer fitted with the paddle attachment, beat SunButter and butter until combined. Scrape down bowl, add the powdered sugar and brown sugar, and beat until combined.

3. Roll 1 teaspoon of mixture into a ball, and place on prepared baking sheet. Continue until all the dough is used. If needed, add more powdered sugar until you reach a consistency that is easy to roll. Place in the freezer for 30 minutes.

4. Melt the chocolate chips in the top of a double-boiler, or in a metal bowl that fits over a pan of lightly simmering water. Stir occasionally until smooth, and remove from heat.

5. Using a toothpick or small fork, dip each chilled SunButter ball into the melted chocolate and place on the prepared baking sheet. Chill in refrigerator until chocolate is set, at least 30 minutes.

6. Serve chilled, and keep leftovers in the refrigerator.

SNICKERDOODLES

G, D, P, TN, S, E, F, SF (8/8)

Another benefit to growing up in 1980s Oklahoma is that my mom and grandmother often used oleo instead of butter. If you don't know what oleo is, just know that you could totally substitute Earth Balance or butter-flavored vegetable shortening and be in business. The point is, this is my mom's recipe, which is naturally dairy-free, since she used that super-trendy oleo. I've made it gluten-free and egg-free, as well. You can always use butter, regular flour, and 2 eggs, if you're not entertaining any allergic types.

PREP TIME: 15 minutes • **CHILL TIME:** 3 hours • **COOK TIME:** 8 minutes • **MAKES:** 24 servings

2 tablespoons golden flax meal

1 cup Earth Balance or butter-flavored vegetable shortening

1¾ cups sugar

1¾ cups all-purpose gluten-free, dairy-free flour

2 teaspoons cream of tartar

1 teaspoon baking soda

½ teaspoon salt

2 teaspoons cinnamon

1. In a small bowl, whisk together flax meal and 6 tablespoons water. Allow to stand for 10 minutes.

2. Using an electric mixer or stand mixer, cream butter substitute or shortening and 1½ cups sugar. Add flax meal and water mixture and combine well. Add flour, cream of tartar, baking soda, and salt, and mix well.

3. Transfer dough to refrigerator and chill for 3 hours or more.

4. Preheat oven to 400°F and prepare baking sheet by lightly spraying with vegetable oil spray.

5. In a small bowl, combine cinnamon and the remaining ¼ cup sugar well.

6. Remove chilled dough from refrigerator and roll dough into balls 1½" to 2" in diameter. Roll balls in cinnamon and sugar mixture and place on baking sheet.

7. Bake for 8 minutes, or until edges are golden brown.

CHOCOLATE BARK

G, D, P, TN, S, E, F, SF (8/8)

One of the easiest and most fancy-looking treats to serve up at the bake sale is chocolate bark, with all kinds of special toppings. While making bark is very easy, making sure it's allergen-free requires a bit of attention to ingredients. To keep your bark eight allergen-free, use dark chocolate and try citrus salts, sunflower seeds, or candied fruits sprinkled on top. Before you begin, check your chocolate bar ingredients, as some can contain barley malt or dairy. If you're using milk chocolate bars, they will not be dairy-free. White chocolate may also contain dairy. Pump up the thickness of the bark by increasing the amount of chocolate you melt, or keep it lean and mean by following the recipe.

PREP TIME: 10 minutes • **COOK TIME:** 7 minutes • **CHILL TIME:** 2 hours • **MAKES:** 24 servings

24 ounces dark chocolate, chopped

Toppings: candied orange slices, sunflower seeds, gluten- and dairy-free pretzels, flavored sea salt

1. Line a baking sheet with wax paper or parchment paper and set aside.

2. Using a double-boiler, or a metal bowl that fits on top of a pot, boil water. Place chocolate in metal bowl or double-boiler top.

3. Stir chocolate to make it smooth as it melts. When it's fully melted, pour evenly onto baking sheet. Use spatula to spread mixture evenly over baking sheet.

4. Sprinkle toppings over different sections of the chocolate. Refrigerate for 2 hours.

5. Remove chocolate from refrigerator and break into pieces.

POPCORN BALLS

G, D, P, TN, S, E, F, SF (8/8)

This is my grandmother's recipe that my mother always made as well, and now I'm carrying on this naturally gluten-free, dairy-free, and every other "-free" treat. If you use butter to shape the balls, this recipe will no longer be dairy-free. Getting out the candy thermometer may seem like a pain, but it's 100 percent worth it to get the precise temperature for this recipe. For holiday bake sales, you can add a few drops of food coloring to get the right holiday hue. I like to dress up popcorn balls with a chocolate drizzle or a quick roll in crushed candies. If those ingredients float your boat, I suggest you do the same.

PREP TIME: 10 minutes • **COOK TIME:** 20 minutes • **MAKES:** 12 balls

12 cups plain popped corn

2 cups sugar

½ cup corn syrup

1 teaspoon apple-cider vinegar

½ teaspoon salt

1 teaspoon vanilla extract

Vegetable oil or Earth Balance

1. Place popcorn in a large bowl and set aside.

2. In a medium saucepan, combine sugar, 1½ cups water, corn syrup, vinegar, and salt and heat on medium-high heat. Continue stirring occasionally until candy thermometer reads 240°F (hard-ball stage). Stir in vanilla and combine well.

3. Pour mixture over popcorn and mix well.

4. Working quickly, use vegetable oil or butter substitute on your hands to help shape popcorn into 3" balls. Place balls on a baking sheet and allow to cool. Caution: Mixture will be hot; do not let little hands help with this step.

SWEET & SAVORY HAND PIES—3 WAYS

G, D, P, TN, S, E, F, SF (8/8)

Since a bake sale can always use a little savory addition, I like to mix it up when I bring hand pies. Since all three fillings are incredibly easy, you can make little batches of them all and show off at drop-off time. Each filling recipe will make 12 to 15 pies, so you will need to double the pie crust allotment, if you're going crazy with all three delicious options. You can either use a pre-made allergy-friendly pie crust for this recipe, or refer back to Chapter 6 and use my Pie Crust (page 80).

PREP TIME: 30 minutes • **COOK TIME:** 25 minutes • **CHILL TIME:** 30 minutes
MAKES: 12 servings

> Gluten-free, dairy-free pie crust, chilled

Pumpkin Filling

> 1 can (15 ounces) pumpkin puree
>
> ¼ cup brown sugar, packed
>
> 2 teaspoons cinnamon
>
> ½ teaspoon nutmeg

In a medium bowl, combine pumpkin, brown sugar, cinnamon, and nutmeg. Set aside.

Spicy Black Bean Filling

> 1 tablespoon olive oil
>
> 1 clove garlic, minced
>
> 1 can (15 ounces) black beans, drained
>
> 1 teaspoon red-pepper flakes
>
> ½ teaspoon salt
>
> ½ teaspoon cumin
>
> 1 teaspoon paprika
>
> ½ teaspoon onion powder

1. Heat oil in medium pan over medium-high heat for 2 minutes. Turn heat down to medium and add garlic. Cook until garlic begins to soften, 3 to 4 minutes.

2. Add black beans, pepper flakes, salt, cumin, paprika, and onion powder and cook for 10 minutes on low heat. Remove from heat and set aside to cool.

Apple Filling

>8 cups (8 fist-size apples) apple chunks, skin on
>1 tablespoon fresh lemon juice
>2 cups brown sugar
>½ cup all-purpose gluten-free, dairy-free flour
>1 teaspoon cinnamon
>Dash of nutmeg

1. In a large bowl, toss apples in lemon juice and set aside.

2. In a Dutch oven, combine 5 cups water and brown sugar, and bring to a light boil.

3. Whisk in flour, cinnamon, and nutmeg, and cook for 1 to 2 more minutes.

4. Add apples to Dutch oven and stir well. Turn heat down to low and cook for 5 minutes.

5. Remove from heat and allow to cool.

After your fillings are made, begin your hand pie construction. If you're making all 3 fillings, you'll need to double the pie crust recipe.

1. Preheat oven to 350°F. Line a baking sheet with parchment paper.

2. Roll out pie crust in a circle on parchment paper. Pie crust should be very thin.

3. Using a paring knife or other small knife, place a small saucer on dough and cut around to create your pie crust.

4. Using a ¼-cup measure or large spoon, cover half of the dough circle with filling, and fold over the other half, creating a half-moon shape. Using a fork, press the edges of the hand pie together and transfer to the prepared baking sheet. Poke 2 or 3 holes into crust. Repeat with remaining dough and filling.

5. Bake pies for 25 minutes, or until well browned.

6. Remove from oven and allow to cool before serving.

MILLET CANDY CRISPY BARS

G, P, TN, S, E, F, SF (7/8)

Ever since Kellogg's took back their gluten-free Rice Krispies (bo-o-o-o-oo!!!!!!), I've been back in the kitchen trying to make fun marshmallow treats that are safe for a variety of people, including me. While millet certainly matches in stickability, the texture is not quite as crispy, so I decided to dress these guys up for the bake sale with a variety of fun candies on top. If you choose candies other than the ones I've listed below, you must look for allergens before declaring them safe for mass consumption.

PREP TIME: 5 minutes • **COOK TIME:** 10 minutes • **COOLING TIME:** 20 minutes • **MAKES:** 24 bars

> 3 tablespoons butter
> 40 large marshmallows or 4 cups miniature marshmallows (1 package)
> 6 cups puffed millet cereal
> Toppings: Pop Rocks, Red Hots, dairy-free chocolate chips

1. Melt butter over medium-high heat in a large saucepan. Add marshmallows and stir until completely melted.

2. Remove mixture from heat and add cereal, stirring to combine completely.

3. Pour mixture into a buttered 13" x 9" pan and, using wax paper, press mixture down and even the top.

4. Allow treats to cool and then cut into rectangles 2" wide and 1" long. Place candy on top to create little bites of awesomeness.

Chapter
8

It's Party Time . . . Excellent!

D o you know what's great about being an adult? When you hear the word "party," you think "wine bong" instead of "birthday cake." Which makes it much easier for those of us with special food needs. Once you reach the legal age, ahem, it's more important what cocktail you're serving up in your punch bowl (which may or may not be a brand-new trash can) than hovering over the birthday candle blow-out scene to guarantee you a good spot for a big slice.

Oh, who am I kidding? The food is the best part of the party no matter if you're celebrating your 9th or 99th birthday. The booze just helps us oldies feel a little bit less stressed when we see puff pastry–wrapped dairy on every hors d'oeuvres platter. Which makes it especially sad for kids who cannot lean on booze to help them through the tough times—those little troopers who show up to celebrate and find out they'll have to suck on ice until they can make an early and polite exit.

Seriously, who am I trying to fool, here? Kids will make the LOUDEST exit possible if they are denied cake, or other special treats at a party. And you know what? I don't blame them. Who wants to be the only kid who isn't allowed to eat one damn thing at the party? If you can show me a kid who happily walks away from bagel bites, pizza rolls, and cake pops followed by cookies and ice cream because that party was OFF THE HOOK—I'll show you a total sociopath.

I don't know about you, but my main goals for my own kids' birthday parties include no vomit and no tears. (Failed at both this year, though.) If I can make up an allergy-friendly dessert that will please everyone involved (and I can, oh, I can), dammit, I'll do it. Kids not only want to fit in but they also want to feel like part of the crowd while eating loads of carbs and sugar. If you want to make sure everyone feels not cheated and properly party-fed, you have to get creative, and you have to be prepared with backup for the allergic kiddo in the crowd. Sure, it's perfectly okay—incredibly kind, even—to provide a gluten-, nut-, and dairy-free cupcake to the kid who can't tolerate any of that biz. And if you walk away from this book only doing that one thing, I would love to hug your neck. Twice, even. But this chapter is about throwing a party and mixing up the allergy-friendly treats so everyone can enjoy the fun without getting sick, or worse, while also making kids who don't have any food issues feel stoked about the goodies coming their way.

Whether you're the parent of or the host of the allergic kid, you want to make sure said kid also doesn't feel like a pariah while chowing down at Billy's bar mitzvah. Which is why I would humbly suggest that you check out some of these allergy-friendly recipes in this chapter and adjust your party menu. Although I'm hoping you checked out the chapter guiding you through bake sales first, because that's where you will find the cake. We all know the centerpiece of the birthday-type party is always going to be the cake, so look there first, or hire a pro to make a kick-ass birthday cake in the shape of whatever your kid is obsessed with now. I'm going to guess based on age.

0–2: Anything cute and furry

3–5: Elmo (runner-up: Thomas the Train and his weird friends)

6–8: LEGOs, Star Wars, American Girl, Pokémon (hopefully not at all the same time)

9–11: Karaoke and pop stars, sports, Mario Bros.

12–18: It's none of your effing business, and stop talking to me!!! Gawd!!!!! (door slam)

Yes, those all make for great cakes, and, if you're feeling not quite up to the task, please reach out to your local baker and order an allergy-friendly version of Elmo/LEGOs/Taylor Swift for your kiddo's best birthday EVER.

Foolproof Party Trick

While I've always been the person who leaves a party and only wants to talk about the food, in today's allergic world, it's far better to make the food a secondary part of your child's celebration, when possible. Especially when there are other kids around who may not benefit from the traditional Oreo ice cream cake you make your daughter every single year, but half of her class is allergic to.

My biggest piece of advice to you (even as I supply you with all of these party food recipes) is to focus on the activity, so the kids won't give a damn about the food. Or will maybe just not care as much, because as I said before, the food RULES. Heading to a theme park or the roller-skating rink means that you don't have to make any food, and you can ask parents of the allergic to provide food due to the restrictions of the venue where the party is being held. It will be a LOAD off your back, and if you don't know how to cook, well, you won't have to cook.

While you may not want to employ the "dazzle them with an expensive party" trick on every playdate, and you still don't want to cook, check out the Resources (page 197) for allergy-friendly pre-packaged snacks. Fill your pantry with these snacks, and serve up seltzer with a dash of fruit juice. Your playdate just got a heckuva lot easier.

But probably the best way to feed children, while also keeping them all safe, is to convince the children that fruit is nature's candy. And not in an ironic way. Because if fruit is your main ingredient, you can mix and match and freeze your way to allergy-free kid-party success. Ice pops are also a fab way to check your vegan and kosher boxes, making fruit-flavored ice pops your go-to dessert no matter the occasion, no matter the guests, no matter the time of year because, come on, ice pops ROCK. And as long as you're not putting meat, bread, or dairy in them (I mean, a "meatsicle" does not exactly scream party, am I right?), you have all eight allergens beaten down, and a sweet vegan and kosher treat, as well. So you master that, then you can hand out delicious homemade ice pops at every kid gathering and safely feed groups! YOU WIN!!!! Pro tip: If you master the ice pop game, the next stop is a food truck or pop-up stand in Austin/Brooklyn/Madison/Boulder/Silver Lake/Portland, and you'll be the hippest mom in town. You're welcome.

VERY IMPORTANT REMINDER!

As I mentioned in the previous chapter, and it bears repeating: Keep your allergy-friendly food safe by not allowing it to mix with the rest of the food. This means that when you prepare it, as it's cooking, and as it's being served up on a My Little Pony plate. If you have a mix of allergy-friendly treats, make party-themed labels that clearly identify the treats so those kids feel special and awesome instead of less-than. Safety first, moms and dads: You don't want any drama at the kid party that doesn't involve who is pro- and who is anti-Bieber.

Now let's have a party! A very safe, but super-awesome party. Huzzah!

ICE POP PARTY!

My friend, former coworker, and food writer extraordinaire (*The Other Side of the Tortilla* is her award-winning blog) Maura Wall Hernandez is an ice pop pro. When I told her about this book and how I firmly believed ice pops would bring all of us food allergy and food issue people together, she not only agreed, she schooled me on the art of ice pop making. At that point, I realized that she was the master, and I the student. Hernandez contributed all of these ice pop recipes, and I just got to enjoy eating them. Who's the master now? Well, it's still her, but if you're looking for the perfect dessert that will please the allergy crowd, you've just found it. Here are five amazing ice pop flavors for your next big blow-out party.

STRAWBERRY LEMONADE ICE POPS

G, D, P, TN, S, E, F, SF (8/8)

This is going to be the ice pop you begin with because everyone freaking loves strawberry lemonade. That's just science. These are also so incredibly easy, you should have your kid do the strawberry hulling to make it even easier on yourself.

PREP TIME: 35 minutes • **FREEZE TIME:** 6 hours • **MAKES:** 10 ice pops

> 1 pound washed, hulled, and sliced strawberries
> ¼ cup pure cane sugar (not refined white sugar)
> ¾ cup fresh-squeezed lemon juice (about 3 large lemons)

1. Put strawberries into a bowl and sprinkle with sugar. Allow to macerate for 30 minutes.

2. Mix lemon juice with ½ cup water, and set aside.

3. Add the strawberries to a blender, pour the lemon juice mixture over the top, and blend on low speed until the strawberries are mostly pureed, but with some small chunks left.

4. Pour into molds, add sticks, and freeze for at least 6 hours, or until frozen solid.

ARNOLD PALMER ICE POPS

G, D, P, TN, S, E, F, SF (8/8)

About a year or so ago, my daughter became obsessed with Arnold Palmers. I realized that this was the start of tweenhood when you could order a drink and feel big. I would highly recommend these at your next tween party, and be sure to pass them out with the proper attitude.

You can use regular lemons or Meyer lemons with this recipe, but if you're using Meyer lemons, reduce sugar to 5 tablespoons.

PREP TIME: 25 minutes • **FREEZE TIME:** 6 hours • **MAKES:** 10 ice pops

> 2 decaf tea bags (I used Lipton decaf tea)
>
> 2 cups hot water
>
> 6 tablespoons pure cane sugar (not refined white sugar)
>
> 1 cup warm water
>
> ¾ cup freshly squeezed lemon juice (about 3 large lemons), pulp reserved

1. Brew tea bags in hot water for 5 to 6 minutes, and then refrigerate for about 15 minutes to bring to room temperature.

2. While the tea is in the refrigerator cooling, dissolve sugar in warm water. Set aside.

3. Combine tea, water and sugar mixture, and lemon juice, adding about 1 tablespoon of the pulp. Stir to mix well.

4. Pour into molds, add sticks, and freeze for 6 hours, or until frozen solid.

MANGO-PINEAPPLE ICE POPS

G, D, P, TN, S, E, F, SF (8/8)

These mango-pineapple guys are going to become your new summer staple. Add chile lime salt, to taste, keeping those little palates in mind. If you're working an older crowd, or even adults, go for that spice for an unforgettable pop. (Psst, adults, maybe enjoy yours with a shot of tequila. All this ice-pop-making means that you deserve a break.)

PREP TIME: 10 minutes • **FREEZE TIME:** 6 hours • **MAKES:** 10 ice pops

1½ cups frozen mango chunks

1¼ cups pineapple juice

10 tablespoons canned crushed pineapple, drained

2–3 tablespoons Tajín or other chile lime salt

1. In a blender, add mango and pineapple juice. Blend on high until fully incorporated.

2. Spoon 1 tablespoon crushed pineapple into the bottom of each mold.

3. Pour the mango-pineapple mixture into molds, add sticks, and freeze for at least 6 hours, or until frozen solid.

4. Sprinkle each ice pop liberally with Tajín or other chile lime salt before serving.

COCONUT CREAM ICE POPS

G, D, P, TN, S, E, F, SF (8/8)

Holy coconut, these are tasty. From the crunchy, toasty coconut pieces to the creamy, sweet flavors, this could quickly become a fan favorite. Note from the chef: While any honey will work in this recipe, high-quality honey makes a lovely, tasty difference. I love Trader Joe's Turkish honey.

PREP TIME: 10 minutes • **FREEZE TIME:** 6 hours • **MAKES:** 10 ice pops

> 1 cup sweetened shredded coconut, toasted
>
> 2 cups canned coconut milk
>
> 1½ cups canned coconut cream
>
> 6 tablespoons honey
>
> 2 teaspoons pure vanilla extract

1. Preheat the oven to 400°F. Spread shredded coconut on a baking sheet and bake for 2 to 3 minutes, until coconut begins to turn golden brown. Remove baking sheet from oven and allow to cool. (You can also use a toaster oven rather than a conventional oven.)

2. In a blender, add coconut milk, coconut cream, honey, and vanilla. Blend on high until all ingredients are fully incorporated.

3. Divide the toasted coconut into the bottom of the molds.

4. Pour the liquid mixture into molds over the toasted coconut, add sticks, and freeze for at least 6 hours, or until frozen solid.

STRAWBERRY CHEESECAKE ICE POPS

G, D, P, E, F, SF (6/8)

Food writer Maura Wall Hernandez made these cheesecake ice pops dairy-free and damned delicious. Her experimenting with the dairy-free options means that soy (in the dairy-free cream cheese) and almonds are present, so save these for your dairy-free guests. From Maura: I tested this recipe with both Califia Farms and Silk brand almond creamers. Almond creamers mimic the texture of heavy cream; mixed with the cream cheese it gives a dense, silky texture. Yummers.

PREP TIME: 30 minutes • **FREEZE TIME:** 6 hours • **MAKES:** 10 ice pops

2½ cups strawberries, washed, hulled, and diced small (about 20 large strawberries)

2½–3 tablespoons pure cane sugar (not white refined sugar)

1 cup nondairy cream cheese

½ cup unsweetened almond milk coffee creamer

2 tablespoons strawberry jam or preserves

1 teaspoon pure vanilla extract

½ cup gluten-free graham cracker crumbs, for dusting/garnish

1. Place the strawberries into a glass bowl and sprinkle with sugar. Allow to macerate for approximately 20 minutes.

2. In a small food processor or blender, add cream cheese, creamer, strawberry jam or preserves, vanilla, and half of the macerated berries. Blend until mostly smooth and all ingredients are fully incorporated.

3. Pour the contents of the food processor into the glass bowl and gently stir with remaining strawberries.

4. Pour into molds, add sticks, and freeze for at least 6 hours, or until frozen solid.

5. Before serving, pour graham cracker crumbs into a dish. Remove ice pops from molds and either sprinkle crumbs on top, or dip the top halves of the ice pops into the crumbs.

SAUSAGE BALLS

G, P, TN, S, E, F, SF (7/8)

My mom always made these around the holidays, but I think they're a great appetizer anytime of the year. While I use Italian sausage (sweet or hot, depending on my mood), I'll always be fond of what my mom used back in the days of the farm—Blue and Gold sausage sold by the local Future Farmers of America. No matter your sausage choice, make sure it's gluten-free, and go for casein-free, if you're feeling very thoughtful or dealing with a dairy allergy. If you're going for dairy-free, substitute Daiya or another vegan cheese for the Cheddar.

PREP TIME: 10 minutes • **COOK TIME:** 20 minutes • **MAKES:** 24 balls

1 cup cooked rice, chilled

1 cup shredded sharp Cheddar cheese

1 pound gluten-free ground sausage

Salt and black pepper

1. Preheat oven to 375°F. Spray a baking sheet with vegetable or olive oil spray and set aside.

2. Combine rice, cheese, sausage, and salt and pepper in a large bowl; you may need to use your hands to thoroughly mix. Shape into 1½" balls and place on the prepared baking sheet.

3. Bake for 20 minutes, or until light brown.

PLAIN OL' GUACAMOLE

G, D, P, TN, S, E, F, SF (8/8)

My 7-year-old informed me that no kids would eat guacamole "with chunks." When he put it that way, well, it made total sense because, chunks. Gross. So I recommend you do what we do at our house when serving up the guac—skip the tomatoes and onions, and keep the ingredients simple. Great with tortilla chips.

PREP TIME: 15 minutes • MAKES: 8 servings

3 ripe avocados

Juice of ½ lemon or lime

½ teaspoon garlic powder

¼ teaspoon onion powder

¼ teaspoon cayenne pepper

½ teaspoon cumin

½ teaspoon paprika

½ teaspoon salt

¼ teaspoon black pepper

Dash of hot sauce

1. Cut avocados in half and remove pits. Remove green avocado meat and place in a serving bowl. Add remaining ingredients and mix until well combined, but not overmixed and liquidy.

2. Serve immediately.

SNACKADIUM

G, P, TN, F, SF (5/8)

Less a recipe and more of an assemblage, Pillsbury released the Snackadium on the world pre–Super Bowl one year, and I thought, "I have to make it gluten-free!!!!" So I did. You can keep it eight main allergen-free by checking your brand of chicken fingers, barbecue sauce, mustard, chips, and bread (see Resources on page 197) and by skipping the cheese. It is no longer soy-free if you use nondairy tofu sour cream. Here's how you do it.

PREP TIME: 30 minutes • **MAKES:** 12 servings

> Plain Ol' Guacamole (page 141)
>
> Sour cream
>
> Baby carrots
>
> Salsa
>
> Tortilla chips
>
> Gluten-free, dairy-free, soy-free chicken fingers (see Resources on page 197)
>
> Barbecue sauce
>
> Mustard
>
> Celery
>
> Hummus
>
> 2 loaves gluten-free, dairy-free, sugar-free French-style bread (see Resources on page 197)
>
> Sandwich meats and fillings

1. Your Snackadium is a snack tray that will resemble a football stadium. The snacks will include guacamole, salsa, tortilla chips, chicken fingers, barbecue sauce, mustard, carrots, celery, hummus, and sandwiches. Yes, you read that right.

2. Spread Plain Ol' Guacamole thinly over a 6-by-10-inch or smaller baking sheet. Using a zip-top bag with a hole cut in one end, draw lines on the "field" with sour cream. Include goalposts. Place carrots around "field" as if they were players.

3. Cut 6 mini-loaf foil pans to resemble stadium seating. Cut the short sides at an angle, and remove the front of one of the long sides and set up around the "field" to allow for spectators. Your spectators include carrot sticks, celery sticks, chicken fingers, and tortilla chips. Fill up those seats with these, standing up as if they were people.

4. Using 4 small bowls or ramekins, fill each with the following condiments: BBQ sauce, mustard, salsa, and hummus. Place in the 4 corners next to the stadium seating.

5. Using 2 large loaves of French-style bread or a reasonable substitute, make 2 large and 4 small submarine sandwiches using ingredients of your choice. Check lunchmeats for any additives. Arrange submarine sandwiches around the edges of your stadium seating and you've got yourself a game.

MAMA'S KICKIN' BLACK BEAN DIP

G, D, P, TN, S, E, F, SF (8/8)

I'm a full-grown adult, but I still admit to picking up the Fritos Bean Dip and going crazy with some chips. It's a delicious savory snack after school or at a party, but not so great for sensitive kids (or anyone, really). A great bean dip that's safe, however, can be a delicious and very popular treat with everyone around the table. While I don't think you should always be sneaking vegetables into kid food, this is one case where it adds nutrition as well as texture—and the little ones will never know the difference. Serve with corn chips, crudités, or even French fries!

PREP TIME: 10 minutes • **COOK TIME:** 35 minutes • **MAKES:** 20 servings

> 2 tablespoons olive oil
>
> 1 yellow onion, chopped
>
> 4 cloves garlic, quartered
>
> 1 jalapeño pepper, seeded and chopped (wear plastic gloves)
>
> 1 sweet potato, cubed
>
> 3 (10-ounce) cans black beans, with liquid
>
> 1 (15-ounce) can fire-roasted diced tomatoes, with juice
>
> 1 teaspoon cumin
>
> 1 teaspoon paprika
>
> 2 teaspoons sea salt
>
> 2 teaspoons black pepper

1. Heat oil on medium-high in a large pot.

2. Add onions, garlic, jalapeños, and sweet potatoes, and cook for 10 minutes, until vegetables are soft.

3. Add beans and tomatoes, with juice, and combine well. Season with cumin, paprika, salt, and pepper, and heat to boiling.

4. Turn heat to low and allow to simmer for 15 minutes.

5. Remove vegetables from heat and allow to cool before blending. Using an immersion blender, blend mixture until smooth, with no lumps.

6. Return to heat and allow to cook on medium for 10 minutes more, until mixture thickens.

RASPBERRY-LIMEADE SORBET

G, D, P, TN, S, E, F, SF (8/8)

I'll admit to having a favorite sorbet, and this is it. It's so refreshing on a hot day and the little kick of lime takes me back to the days of pulling into Sonic and ordering up a limeade. Good times, people. Good times.

PREP TIME: 15 minutes • **COOK TIME:** 5 minutes + about 15 minutes in ice-cream maker
FREEZE TIME: 2 hours • **MAKES:** 16 servings

   1 cup sugar
   6 cups fresh raspberries
   Juice of 2 limes

1. In a large saucepan over high heat, bring sugar and 1 cup water to boil and stir occasionally until sugar dissolves completely. Remove from heat and allow syrup to cool.

2. Add ¾ cup water and raspberries to a blender or food processor, and blend until smooth. Using a very fine strainer or sieve, pour raspberry mixture into strainer over a large bowl. Using a spoon or spatula, push mixture through strainer to extract as much strained raspberry mixture as you can.

3. Add cooled syrup and lime juice to mixture and mix well.

4. Pour mixture into an ice-cream maker and freeze according to manufacturer's directions. Once it's reached desired texture, transfer to an airtight container and freeze for at least 2 hours.

5. Remove sorbet from the freezer, allow to soften slightly, and serve.

BLUEBERRY-BASIL SORBET

G, D, P, TN, S, E, F, SF (8/8)

You can feel good about serving up all the berries to the kids and watching them suck down those antioxidants. I love the little kick of basil in this recipe, but if you have kids who might react to anything green, feel free to skip it.

PREP TIME: 15 minutes • **COOK TIME:** 5 minutes + 15 minutes in ice-cream maker
FREEZE TIME: 2 hours • **MAKES:** 16 servings

> 1 cup water
> 1½ cups sugar
> 5 cups blueberries
> ½ cup lemon juice
> 2 tablespoons chopped fresh basil
> Basil leaves, for garnish (optional)

1. In a large saucepan over high heat, bring water and sugar to boil, and stir occasionally until sugar dissolves completely.

2. Remove from heat and add blueberries, lemon juice, and chopped basil. Stir to mix thoroughly. Let mixture cool for 10 minutes.

3. Transfer mixture to blender or food processor and blend until very smooth.

4. Using a very fine strainer or sieve, pour blueberry/basil mixture into strainer over a large bowl. Using a spoon or spatula, push mixture in strainer to extract as much strained blueberry mixture as you can.

5. Pour mixture into an ice-cream maker, and freeze according to manufacturer's directions. Once it's reached desired texture, transfer to an airtight container and freeze for at least 2 hours.

6. Remove sorbet from the freezer and allow to soften slightly and serve. Add basil leaves, if desired.

DR. PEPPER SORBET

G, D, P, TN, S, E, F, SF (8/8)

Growing up in Oklahoma and Texas means I'm a Pepper. Which is why I thought a great party treat would be this sorbet. My kids lose their minds when I make this, and yours probably will, too. Yes, Dr. Pepper is sweet enough already, but adding in the sugar helps with the texture.

PREP TIME: 5 minutes • CHILL TIME: 20 minutes • MAKES: 8 servings

> 4 tablespoons sugar
> Juice of 1 lemon
> 32 ounces chilled Dr. Pepper
> Maraschino cherries, for garnish

1. In a medium bowl, mix sugar and lemon juice together until sugar is dissolved. Add soda and combine.

2. Pour mixture into ice-cream machine and mix until reaching the proper texture—approximately 20 minutes.

3. Transfer mixture into a sealable container and store in the freezer.

4. Let it thaw a little bit before you scoop to serve and add a cherry on top.

BERRY YOGURT DROPS

G, P, TN, S, E, F, SF (7/8)

Kids are notorious snackers. Those little dudes and dudettes can destroy a bowl of anything in 30 seconds flat. Which is why something relatively good for them piled in a bowl makes a heckuva lot of sense whether after school, during a playdate, or as a belly-filler before the birthday cake comes out. These yogurt drops could not be easier to make, and you can just pull them out of the freezer before serving and let those little hands grab them all up before they melt. DONE.

PREP TIME: 15 minutes • **FREEZE TIME:** 3 hours • **MAKES:** 50 drops

¼ cup fresh raspberries, strawberries, or blueberries

16 ounces vanilla yogurt

2 teaspoons powdered sugar

1. If using strawberries, hull them first. Wash berries and pulse in a food processor or blender until smooth. Add yogurt and powdered sugar, and mix to completely combine.

2. Using an icing bag or a zip-top bag with the corner cut off, fill bag with yogurt mixture.

3. Make ¼" to ½" dots on a parchment paper-covered baking sheet, spaced closely together. Freeze for at least 3 hours.

4. Remove drops from baking sheet and place in bowl to serve.

GUACAMOLE PEPPER BITES

G, D, P, TN, S, E, F, SF (8/8)

As parents, we know that peppers have a load of vitamins and minerals and are super-good for our little snappers. We also know that peppers can be a hard sell to the under-18 set. For some reason, my youngest LOVES red and yellow bell peppers, so I make this easy treat to fancy up my Plain Ol' Guacamole.

PREP TIME: 20 minutes • **MAKES:** 16 servings

4 bell peppers

Plain Ol' Guacamole (page 141)

1. De-stem bell peppers and cut them into quarters. Set aside.

2. Scoop guacamole into pepper "boats," and serve.

SPICY BUFFALO WINGS

G, P, TN, S, E, F, SF (7/8)

PREP TIME: 5 minutes • **CHILL TIME:** 1 hour • **COOK TIME:** 15 minutes • **MAKES:** 20 wings

20 chicken wings

1 cup all-purpose gluten-free flour

½ teaspoon paprika

½ teaspoon cayenne pepper

½ teaspoon salt

½ cup butter

½ cup hot sauce

2 teaspoons black pepper

2 teaspoons garlic powder

About 4 cups vegetable oil, for deep-frying

1. Using a large metal bowl, place chicken wings evenly around bowl and set aside.

2. Whisk together flour, paprika, cayenne pepper, and salt in a small bowl. Sprinkle over the wings and cover. Refrigerate mixture for 1 hour.

3. In a small saucepan, melt butter on medium heat. Add hot sauce, pepper, and garlic powder, and mix completely. Remove from heat and set aside.

4. In a deep skillet or deep-fryer, heat oil on medium-high. Test for readiness by sprinkling water to see if it "dances" on the oil.

5. Working in batches, fry wings in oil for 10 to 15 minutes, turning frequently. Remove wings from skillet and drain on a paper towel-lined plate.

6. When all wings are cooked, transfer them to a medium bowl. Pour sauce over top and mix well.

7. Serve on a platter with your favorite dipping sauce (we like ranch, but the tradition is blue cheese dressing), crudité, or alone.

SPICY VEGAN CAULIFLOWER BUFFALO "WINGS"

G, D, P, TN, S, E, F, SF (8/8)

The vegan alternative is made the same way as the Spicy Buffalo Wings recipes (opposite), but you substitute cauliflower, vegetable oil, and serve it with a dairy-free dip, as well as give it a final heat-up in the oven. Mix and match if food issues are not a problem, otherwise keep these party treats separate on the tray for a dairy-safe snack.

PREP TIME: 5 minutes • **STANDING TIME:** 30 minutes • **COOK TIME:** 25 minutes
MAKES: 20 wings

> 1 head cauliflower, cut into bite-size pieces
> 1 cup all-purpose gluten-free, dairy-free flour
> ½ teaspoon paprika
> ½ teaspoon cayenne pepper
> ½ teaspoon salt
> 3 cups vegetable oil, for deep-frying, plus ½ cup
> ½ cup hot sauce
> 2 teaspoons black pepper
> 2 teaspoons garlic powder

1. Using a large metal bowl, place cauliflower bites evenly around bowl.

2. Whisk together flour, paprika, cayenne pepper, and salt in a small bowl. Sprinkle over the cauliflower and cover. Let stand for 30 minutes.

3. In a deep skillet or deep-fryer, heat 3 cups oil on medium-high heat. Test for readiness by sprinkling water to see if it "dances" on the oil. Preheat oven to 450°F.

4. Working in batches, fry cauliflower in oil for 5 to 8 minutes, turning frequently. Remove cauliflower from skillet and drain on a paper towel–lined plate. Then transfer to a mixing bowl.

5. While cauliflower is frying, heat ½ cup oil on medium heat in a small saucepan. Add hot sauce, black pepper, and garlic powder and mix completely. Pour sauce over top and mix well. Pour onto a baking sheet and bake for 10 minutes, stirring twice.

6. Serve with your favorite dairy-free dipping sauce, crudités, or alone.

VEGGIE TEMPURA

G, D, P, TN, S, E, F, SF (8/8)

Another great way to get kids to eat their veggies is to fry 'em up tempura-style, and add some wheat-free tamari (includes soy) and wasabi for dipping. It's an easy recipe to make gluten-free, as the rice flour is nice and light. If you want the vegetables softer for smaller mouths, you can blanch them ahead of time. Although the mushrooms will be soft enough.

PREP TIME: 20 minutes • **COOK TIME:** 15 minutes • **MAKES:** 24 servings

> 1 cup broccoli florets
> 1 cup sliced sweet potato
> 1 cup sliced yellow squash
> ½ cup mushrooms, sliced
> ½ cup cornstarch
> 4 cups vegetable oil
> 2 cups rice flour
> 1 tablespoon sesame oil
> ½ teaspoon baking soda
> 1½ cups ice-cold water

1. Prepare your workstations first, so the batter does not get too warm. Place vegetables in 1 bowl or on a large plate next to a plate of cornstarch.

2. Heat vegetable oil in a large and deep skillet on high until a sprinkle of water begins to "dance" on surface. Reduce heat to medium-high.

3. In a medium bowl, quickly mix flour, sesame oil, baking soda, and water. Do not overmix.

4. Working quickly, dredge vegetables in cornstarch, and then dunk into batter to completely cover. Cook in batches, being careful not to crowd, for 30 seconds to 1 minute per side.

5. Drain cooked vegetables on a paper towel-lined plate.

SPARKLY JELL-O SALAD

G, D, P, TN, S, E, F, SF (8/8)

We decided to see what would happen if we went full-on retro with a classic Jell-O fruit mold. I suppose it does skip a generation, because our kids went crazy when we presented them with fruit inside Jell-O. You can use a square pan, trifle dish, a Bundt pan, a fun cake pan, or anything else that screams "fun." Bring this retro dessert out at your next party, and it will be an allergy-friendly hit. (Hint: You can get vegan gelatin at certain markets, if you have vegans in the house.)

PREP TIME: 15 minutes • **COOK TIME:** 10 minutes • **CHILL TIME:** 4 hours • **MAKES:** 12 servings

> 2 packages Berry Blue Jell-O
> ½ cup sparkling lemon-lime drink (7-Up, Sprite)
> ½ cup allergy-free jelly beans (see Resources on page 197)
> 1 cup washed, hulled, and sliced strawberries

1. Empty both Jell-O packets into a large bowl and set aside.

2. In a medium saucepan, bring 3 cups water to a boil. Pour over Jell-O and stir quickly to completely dissolve.

3. Add sparkling drink and stir. Continue to stir until mixture begins to thicken.

4. Pour half of Jell-O mixture into mold. Layer half of candy and half of fruit. Pour remaining Jell-O into mold and layer remaining candy and fruit.

5. Allow mixture to set in the refrigerator for at least 4 hours before serving.

TACO PIE

G, P, TN, S, E, F, SF (7/8)

Perhaps you're sensing a theme here. Yes, it involves tacos and delicious Mexican food. Since traditional Mexican dishes, and some nontraditional Mexican dishes, are naturally allergen-free, they're a good go-to when you're not sure what else to feed a hungry, allergic crowd. This incredibly easy Taco Pie is essentially a mash-up between shepherd's pie and taco meat. It's everything kids love (taco meat, mashed potatoes, cheese) in one pie! If you want to make it dairy-free, skip the milk and butter. Try to use a small amount of coconut milk or rice milk to make your potatoes creamy. You can top with something other than cheese as well, or sprinkle with nutritional yeast.

PREP TIME: 10 minutes • COOK TIME: 1 hour • MAKES: 12 servings

> 3 large russet potatoes, peeled and quartered
>
> 1 pound ground beef
>
> 3 teaspoons chili powder
>
> ¼ teaspoon garlic powder
>
> ¼ teaspoon onion powder
>
> ¼ teaspoon oregano
>
> ¼ teaspoon paprika
>
> ¼ teaspoon cumin
>
> ½ teaspoon salt, plus more as needed
>
> ½ teaspoon black pepper, plus more as needed
>
> 4 tablespoons butter
>
> ½ cup milk
>
> ½ cup shredded Cheddar cheese
>
> ½ cup shredded Monterey Jack cheese

1. Preheat oven to 350°F. Coat a pie plate with olive or vegetable oil spray.

2. Boil 6 cups water in a large pot. Add potatoes and boil until a fork can easily slide into potatoes.

3. Brown ground beef in a large skillet over medium heat. Drain grease, and stir in chili powder, garlic powder, onion powder, oregano, paprika, cumin, salt, and pepper. Reduce heat to low and cook for 5 minutes more. Remove from heat.

4. Drain the potatoes and return them to pot. Over low heat, add butter and milk, and mash potatoes until smooth. Add a dash of salt and pepper, to taste, and remove from heat.

5. Fill prepared pan with seasoned meat. Cover completely with mashed potatoes and bake for 30 minutes.

6. After 30 minutes, remove pie from oven and cover with cheeses. Bake for 15 minutes more.

7. Remove from oven and serve by the slice.

SWEET & SPICY PEAS

G, D, P, TN, S, E, F, SF (8/8)

Yes, I do really believe that you can get kids to snack on peas at a party. Especially if you throw them down on a table while kids have their eyes glued to the latest Disney flick. While some kids would love those wasabi peas you can pick up at Trader Joe's, this is a milder, and allergy-free, version.

PREP TIME: 10 minutes • **COOK TIME:** 15 minutes • **MAKES:** 20 servings

½ cup granulated sugar

¼ cup brown sugar

2 tablespoons hot water

1 tablespoon hot sauce

3 cups fresh green peas

Sprinkle of cayenne pepper

1. In a medium bowl, combine granulated sugar, brown sugar, water, and hot sauce.

2. Add peas and mix until evenly coated.

3. Heat vegetable oil on medium high heat in large skillet.

4. Working in batches, fry peas, stirring frequently until crisp (3 to 5 minutes per batch).

5. Remove peas from skillet and drain on a paper towel-lined plate.

6. Sprinkle with cayenne pepper and serve.

CHOCOLATE COCONUT PANNA COTTA

G, D, P, TN, S, E, F, SF (8/8)

Panna cotta is a fancy name for pudding, and this recipe is a fancy way to make it eight main allergen-free. If your party is attended by adults, feel free to sprinkle some sweetened coconut flakes on top. But if you have kids with texture issues (which is to say, most kids), skip that flourish.

PREP TIME: 10 minutes • **COOK TIME:** 10 minutes • **CHILL TIME:** 3 hours • **MAKES:** 10 servings

> 2 packets unflavored gelatin
> 6 tablespoons cold water
> 3 cups coconut cream
> ½ cup sugar
> 8 ounces dark chocolate, chopped into 1" pieces, plus more for shaving
> ¼ teaspoon vanilla extract
> Dash of salt

1. Combine gelatin and water in a small bowl. Set aside to rest.

2. Heat coconut cream and sugar in a small saucepan over low heat to a simmer until sugar dissolves. Whisk in chocolate and stir until melted.

3. Add vanilla and salt, and mix thoroughly.

4. Remove mixture from heat and add gelatin mixture. Mix thoroughly and transfer to 8 ramekins or 1 quiche dish.

5. Refrigerate for at least 3 hours.

6. Serve with chocolate shavings on top.

POM-ORANGE SPARKLY PUNCH

G, D, P, TN, S, E, F, SF (8/8)

I miss the ginger ale-spiked punch of my youth, so I like to re-create it when we have kiddos over who've never known the joy of a punch-bowl drink that puts fizz up your nose. It also gives me an excuse to dust off the punch bowl and ladle and pretend it's the 1950s. You do that, too, right?

PREP TIME: 10 minutes • **MAKES:** 12 servings

3 cups no-pulp orange juice

2 cups pomegranate juice

3 cups ginger ale

2–4 cups ice

6 orange slices

1. Combine orange juice and pomegranate juice in a large punch bowl and mix well. Stir in ginger ale.

2. Add ice to fill one-quarter of the bowl.

3. Top with orange slices and serve.

STRAWBERRY LEMONADE

G, D, P, TN, S, E, F, SF (8/8)

A perennial favorite, we like to keep the strawberry lemonade on hand at my house. It's a great party drink for kids and adults alike. Feel free to experiment with other types of berries, but we keep coming back to this classic version.

PREP TIME: 20 minutes • **COOK TIME:** 5 minutes • **CHILL TIME:** 30 minutes
MAKES: 15 servings

> 2 cups sugar
> 20 strawberries, washed and hulled
> 1½ cups fresh lemon juice (about 10 lemons)
> Strawberries and lemon slices, for garnish

1. In a small saucepan, mix 1½ cups sugar with 1 cup water and heat until sugar is completely dissolved. Remove from heat and allow to cool to room temperature. Then transfer to refrigerator and cool for 30 minutes.

2. Combine strawberries and the remaining ½ cup sugar in a blender to liquefy mixture. Scrape down the sides and transfer to a medium bowl.

3. Combine cooled sugar water, lemon juice, and 7 cups water in a large pitcher and mix well. Add strawberry mixture and stir until completely combined.

4. Garnish with strawberries and lemon slices and serve over ice.

Chapter
9

Have Life-Saving Drugs, Will Travel

Now that you've made every single recipe in this book and are enjoying an allergy-free lifestyle, girl, you need a vacation. No matter how scary that may seem with an allergic kid in tow, it's not only possible, it's required, so you don't lose your damn mind. Vacations are where family memories are made, yes, even the bad ones. They are an important rite of passage, even if it's just a long weekend a short drive away. Once you've gotten used to your lifestyle change with a food-allergic kid in your house, it's time to explore beyond those four walls. Don't worry, I'm going to walk/drive/fly you through it.

Depending on your child's allergy, and depending on your own wildest vacation desires, you may want to start small or jump right into the vacation of your dreams. While I wouldn't necessarily recommend a family trip to Iceland with your fish-allergic kid, you may be able to pack enough allergy-free snacks and book an apartment with a kitchenette and make it work. It won't be the first time a kid lives on grilled cheese sandwiches while on vacation, and certainly wouldn't be the last. It's all about your own comfort zone, and always keeping an eye on your child's health. (Note: *Health* refers to the allergy only while on vacation. Ice cream and candy consumption while taking a trip does not work against the kid whose only issue is shellfish.)

Much like every damn thing in life, the secret to having a great time and doing it right is to prepare, prepare, and prepare some more. If you do your prep work early on and thoroughly, you can relax a bit while you're on vacation with your family of five. Hahahahaha! I just said "relax" and "family of five" in the same sentence. Still, relaxish.

Google It

Yes, that is a very lazy way for me to give you a piece of advice, but it's the best advice ever. And something I do before I ever leave home for my next great gluten-free adventure. Before you head anywhere on planet Earth, go to your favorite search engine and type in "gluten/dairy/peanut/tree nut/soy/egg/shellfish/fish-free Bogotá" or wherever your adventures may take you. You will find a blogger who has been there, and lived to tell the tale.

Some of my favorite gluten-free restaurants in foreign countries came about because of the old Google trick, and I know I've guided travelers to some great restaurants around the world as well. In addition to checking out the allergy blogs (see Resources on page 197), just run a search and take some notes.

Pack It, Ask It, Just Do It

This may just be me, but I do get nostalgic about packing up ham sandwiches and sodas in an ice-filled cooler and hitting the road. Sure, I get just as nostalgic about hitting the Taco Bell drive-thru, but Taco Bell and I can no longer be friends. Make some memories with your family by packing up your lunches and snacks and taking a road trip. Heck, even if you're flying, it pays to pack a lunch and buy your beverages at the terminal after going through the humiliation that is modern airport security. If you know you have food to feed everyone, especially those with the food allergies, you're well on your way to relaxing into your vacation.

I'm about to lay some theme parks and restaurants (see Resources on page 197) on you that are allergy-friendly. You may get pretty darned excited and start planning your trip right away, but first, I must remind you that even when you're visiting the most allergy-friendly locations (Disney World, I'm looking at you), your allergic kid is still at risk for cross-contact with allergens. What this means for the severely allergic is to not forget those EpiPens, and proceed with caution. Pack plenty of snacks in case things seem to be going sideways when you're ordering food, and be sure to treat your allergic kid to whatever she wants if she gets turned away from a meal more than once. It's about making it magical for everyone, you guys, and sometimes, that means getting spoiled with a nonallergic dessert. Over and over. And over, again. Even allergic adults need to wallow in their limited options, says the woman who gave up and had gelato every morning for breakfast while visiting Paris.

Get out there, you guys! I know a family who took their kid with a severe peanut allergy to China, and they navigated it perfectly. It can be done, no matter how insurmountable the challenge may seem. At the risk of sounding like a former United States Secretary of Defense during the second Gulf War, embrace the unknown, and know the known. Do your research, pack up the allergy-free goodies, and take off.

Kid-Friendly US Destinations

After you take all of this advice under consideration, you may decide to play it safe and only camp out in your backyard. That, my friends, is an absolutely safe and fun vacation destination. The only bummer being that you'll still wind up doing dishes and yelling at your kids to get off screens when they sneak inside to play Wii U. There are other places you can go in the United States that won't require the research and preparation an international vacation will, and you should try those out first before you go global.

National Parks

Having recently been on a tour of several national parks, the main reason I recommend these trips is because our national parks are amazing, and you can bring a picnic lunch wherever you go. While every lodging option will be different depending on the location, check out the allergy-friendly packaged foods and snacks (see Resources on page 197), pack up your favorites, and hit the open road. Being fully prepared with delicious snacks and chain restaurant recommendations (see Resources on page 197), combined with the beautiful vistas you're about to see, will allow you to truly relax and enjoy the view. You can camp out, find a local motel, or do a drive-by. It's one of the most affordable ways to vacation with your family and will be a truly life-changing experience.

Universal Studios: Orlando and Hollywood

If you have a Harry Potter fan in your house, most likely you'll wind up at Hogwart's sooner rather than later. It is a magical place, but not one without its allergens. Having been to both parks (I'm totally sending Harry Potter's kids to college), I would highly recommend that you take your allergic kiddos to the Orlando park if you have a geographic choice. While both parks have the policy of speaking to the servers and chefs to find out allergy-free options, I personally found the staff to be much more responsive in Orlando and the options to be much more extensive as well. While in the park, I found multiple places to enjoy a meal or a snack, but while in Hollywood, it was much safer for me to dine on the Universal CityWalk, outside of the park. Or maybe just more delicious, because the gluten-free pasta at Luigi's in Springfield made me sad.

My feeling is since Universal Orlando is so much bigger than the Hollywood location, and since it was built as a kid-friendly venue instead of an extension of an actual working studio, everything was built with kids in mind. As a season pass holder to Universal Hollywood, it clearly hasn't stopped me from enjoying Butter Beer or a bunless Krusty Burger. You can eat safely there as well; it's just a bit more limited than its Floridian cousin.

Walt Disney World versus Disneyland

Luckily, for those of us with food issues, Walt Disney World introduced new allergy-friendly menus in 2015. In addition to the lovely gluten-free, dairy-free, vegan bakery, Erin McKenna's, you can dine safely throughout the park. Not to be outdone by the likes of me and this book, Disney World covers even more allergens and dietary preferences within their restaurants and food stands. They can, and do, prepare food that is free of gluten or wheat, lactose or milk, peanuts and tree nuts, shellfish, soy, fish, eggs, and corn. Simply let the server know that you have a food allergy, and you will be able to speak with the chef or a food specialist to discuss your safe options. This goes for the resorts on the property, too, so when you order room service, totally get the allergy-free options. Pretty cool, guys.

Disneyland has the same policy of speaking to the server and/or chef when you have a food allergy, but as someone who lives within driving distance of the 'Land, I have to say it's a bummer that I don't see the same options in both parks. Again, I'm thinking it's based on the scale of the operation where, like Universal Studios, the bigger amusement parks have more people to feed, and more food issues to tackle. Therefore, the quantity is going to be greater in the Orlando park. Still, I don't go hungry when I go to Disneyland, and neither will your allergic kid. Don't forget, you may pack your own lunch at these parks as well. I would at least recommend taking a few snacks to make your trip to the happiest place on Earth even happier.

Interestingly, the resort hotels at Disneyland were super-duper on the allergy-friendly front when I've stayed overnight. Those gluten-free Mickey waffles won me over, and the hotel staff all seemed to be on point.

Disney Aulani Hawaii Resort and Spa

A true vacation for both parents and kids, the Disney Aulani located in Ko Olina, Hawaii, is set up to accommodate those with food allergies in two of its restaurants, the 'Ama 'Ama and the Makahiki. Specifically, the chefs are able to prepare safe foods for those who need to be free of gluten or wheat, lactose or dairy, peanuts, tree nuts, shellfish, soy, fish, eggs, and corn. If you have allergies outside of these nine, or if you have multiple allergies, the Aulani advises you to contact the resort at least 14 days ahead of your trip to discuss accommodations for your diet. Other special meals are also available, such as vegetarian, low-sugar, kosher, and more. You can also bring your own food into the Aulani, so pack those snacks!

According to the Disney Aulani, you can fully enjoy the Hawaiian food experience, even with food allergies. Also, according to all of these food bloggers I see getting sent on these trips to show how kid- and allergy-friendly the

Aulani is, it sounds amazing. Not that I'm bitter or anything about never being invited on the blog trips, especially since I've never even been to Hawaii. Not bitter at all. Whatevs, Disney. It's cool; I'm sure you can get allergy-friendly poi anywhere.

Busch Gardens

The Busch Gardens family of amusement parks pride themselves on being able to serve the allergic safely with allergy-free options around the parks and educated staff members to help guide your allergic little one safely. You can hit Busch Gardens, SeaWorld, Sesame Place, Discovery Cove, Aquatica, Adventure Island, and Water Country USA and find someone to help you navigate your lunch spots. Busch Gardens Tampa has an extra bonus for those wanting to get their allergy-safe eat on: a designated restaurant that specializes in keeping your meal safe. Check out Zambia Smokehouse for full-service, allergy-safe dining.

SeaWorld

Part of the Busch Gardens family, you won't want to take your fish-allergic kiddo here. Kidding! You don't actually eat the attractions, although I do find it odd when fish is served at an aquarium. But that's not an allergy issue. While many people have moral objections to attending SeaWorld, it won't be because of the food. In addition to offering packaged snacks that are allergy-friendly, SeaWorld has been working with the Food Allergy and Anaphylaxis Network (FAANTM) to educate their food service staff on how to safely prepare and serve food to those with allergies. Additionally, they have a "Chef's Card"[1] you can download before your trip and hand to everyone who is preparing your food.

Las Vegas

Vegas is basically an adult playground, which is also now somehow family-friendly. Ignore the prostitutes (who do seem to blend in nicely with the scenery), and pick a hotel that is known for kid activities, and you'll be set. A resort city, Las Vegas is hypersensitive to special dietary needs, and you'll find a well-educated staff almost everywhere you dine. Before you book a room, be sure to call ahead to ask about in-room dining options for your allergic kiddo, and if that's not panning out, book a room with a kitchenette. The number of chain and local restaurants may just outnumber the big winners in Vegas, and most of them know how to handle guests with allergies (see Resources on page 197). There are a lot of businesses catering to the allergic in Las Vegas, and you can always pick up dinner or make dinner yourselves before hitting the bright lights.

For the Cruising Families

Personally, the idea of being on a boat far from land panics the celiac in me, but people apparently do this ALL THE TIME. There are definite upsides to taking your family on a cruise, mostly the thing about how your kids will have built-in entertainment 24/7. For anyone who's been on a road trip to a national park, you'll immediately see the value in that. But boarding a boat and being taken far away from a Whole Foods means that you need to do a lot of planning, and a lot of research on which cruise lines are more accommodating for the families dealing with food allergies. Here are a few good options.

Disney Cruise Line

Can we all just agree that Disney has a lock on family- and allergy-friendly entertainment? God help the parents of kids who only have eyes for Dream-Works. Did you know Disney even has its own private Disney island in the Bahamas? Dang, Disney. You're solid. If you're stuck on a cruise ship (ports excluded), you want to make sure your kiddo can eat safely.

While the quick snack joints and room service do not have special-diet options, the restaurants on board Disney cruise ships do offer gluten-free, dairy-free, vegetarian, and no-sugar-added meals. In the case of other severe food allergies, they recommend that you contact the ship before you travel to discuss your child's specific needs. They also recommend that you speak with your head server, and anyone else who comes in contact with your food. I would definitely have a come-to-Jesus conversation before you book, because while Disney does state they will do everything possible to keep your food safe from allergens, they do say it could come into contact with the allergen at some point, since there are no separate facilities for allergy-free food prep. Again, bring snacks and staples, and know before you go.

Royal Caribbean

Some Royal Caribbean ships are more kid-friendly than others, so make sure you're choosing the right one for your family before you book it. And then make sure you fill out your personal profile describing your dietary needs at least 45 days before traveling. You can also email special_needs@rccl.com and let them know, in detail, what kind of food your allergic kiddo requires. You will need to include guests' names, booking number, ship name, and sail date. With all of that said, they can, and do, accommodate food allergies, gluten-free, low-fat, low-sodium, and kosher meal requests. (Kosher note: If you're traveling during Passover, please alert the ship of your kosher for Passover dietary needs 90 days ahead of your travel date.)

Carnival Cruises

In addition to the myriad of activities Carnival has for young and old, they are also up on the special dietary needs tip. As always, you need to contact the ship before you leave and fill them in on what food allergies you will need accommodations for, and if you are specifically needing kosher or Indian vegetarian, you need to contact them at least 2 weeks in advance so they can have your meals ready when you board. There are several gluten-free options on board including breads, rolls, and pizza crusts, so your wheat and gluten kiddo should be set. For other food allergies, the main dining rooms are the only places that will be safe for your kids. As always, speak with your server right away when you sit down to dine.

What's Not Included

You may be wondering why I didn't include some of your favorite family fun spots such as Six Flags. That's because not only does Six Flags not offer allergy-friendly foods, they don't allow you to bring in your own food without a doctor's note. If your kid is bent on going to Six Flags, she's probably old enough to understand how to take care of herself. Still, grab a doctor's note and a picnic before you allow her to jump on the Viper.

The San Diego Zoo is another world-class kid-friendly destination that is not able to accommodate your allergic eaters. Luckily, it's an activity you can do in a matter of hours, and not days, so you'll have time to plan your meals around your zoo adventure and eat off-site. Also, don't you feel better eating somewhere that animals aren't caged up? Just sayin'.

Getting There Is Not Even Half the Fun

B. K. (before kids), flying was a fun adventure that unplugged you from the rest of the world, at least while you were in the air. Now, it's your basic nightmare filled with begging, complaining, and trips to the bathroom. And that's just the annoying guy in the middle seat.

There are no allergy-free airlines, just as there is no allergy-free world. Most airlines don't serve peanuts due to the raised awareness of the severity of peanut allergies, but no airlines guarantee that products with peanuts will not find their way onto your flight. There are precautions some airlines do take, however, and some go further than others. Like anywhere you travel outside of your own home, you have to be ready to communicate your needs clearly, and to anyone who will come into contact with food or drinks the allergic will be consuming.

While I've never gone through the rigmarole of calling ahead to talk about food allergies on a specific flight, my guess is that you'll get varying responses depending on whom you get on the phone. That is why it's a good idea to do as Southwest Airlines suggests and, in addition to letting the airline know when you book your flight that you have a severe allergy, get to the airport early on the day of your flight to make sure that the crew that day is also aware. Southwest also suggests taking a morning flight, when the airplane has been recently cleaned, versus an evening one, when it's been through a day of travel.

United also wants an early heads-up and a heads-up again on the day of travel. For a severe allergy, they will ask people in your immediate area to refrain from eating the offending allergen, but there is no rule against your neighbor being uncooperative (my word, not theirs). JetBlue has a similar policy of creating a "buffer" of the row in front and row behind the allergy sufferer for a severe allergy. They have the added insurance of refunding your ticket if they cannot provide a safe space. Alaska Airlines also cannot guarantee an allergy-free flight and advises you to speak with your doctor before flying. Additionally, Alaska Airlines adds, "Please advise the gate agent if you would like to preboard to cleanse your immediate seating area." Delta Airlines also asks that you request a cleaning of your area before your flight, but specifically refers to peanut allergies. Be sure you have some documentation from a physician if it's nonpeanut related, as the policy is specific to peanuts. Delta will also ask that no peanuts be served at all on the flight if you have a severe allergy. Again, they only refer to peanuts in this instance, but it's worth making some phone calls and finding the right person to talk with if you have a severe allergy to a food that could likely be smeared on your seat from a previous flight.

American Airlines does offer special meals for dietary needs if you call at least 24 hours in advance, but if you aren't on a flight that includes a meal, or if your dietary need is for something other than vegan, gluten-free, diabetes-friendly, kosher, or observant Muslim food, you're out of luck. In the case of nut allergies, American does not allow you to wipe down your own area before a flight, nor do they provide a buffer zone, or any guarantee that products with peanut oil, or any tree nuts, will not be on a flight.

Because Air Canada is as conscientious as the good people of The North (what do they know that we don't???), their policies are not dramatically different than these other airlines', but they are more thorough in their care for people with severe peanut and tree-nut allergies. Children who have a severe food allergy are not allowed to travel as unaccompanied minors, and in addition to the buffer zone of no peanuts or tree nuts, they want to make sure that you know to have your EpiPen on board.

While taking a lot of precautions will keep your kid safe on an airplane, the bottom line is that you must be proactive and not expect an airline to step in and take care of your child's safety. Always remember that your child takes a risk whenever he leaves the safety of your home. You can't keep him in that bubble, no matter how much better it would be for your peace of mind. Prepare, put your oxygen mask on first, and fly away on a family vacation.

Come On, Ride the Train

Amtrak rides seem so romantic, don't they? Maybe romantic isn't the right word when you're traveling with kids, but there still is something very special about seeing the country as you ride along in a train car. Kids will certainly get a kick out of what could be a once-in-a-lifetime experience, so you don't want anyone getting ill while you ride the rails.

Amtrak dining only accommodates a few special diets, unfortunately. Since the meals are made off-site, there is no room for substitutions or adjustments, and they cannot guarantee an allergen-free dining car. Still, if your child has a dairy or egg allergy, you're in luck, as they serve vegan meals with 72 hours' notice before your trip. Kosher meals are also available, if you contact Amtrak within 72 hours of your departure as well. But if your child has any other food allergy, you need to pack your own food to make sure she can safely enjoy breakfast, lunch, and dinner. And don't forget those EpiPens and extra Benadryl in case things do go awry.

Shipping Them Off

If you have a kid who has been begging to go to sleep-away camp, you have probably spent many sleepless nights freaking out about what could go wrong. This is normal, even for those of us who have kids without food issues, but intensified when you're talking about severe allergies. While so many camps are hip to keeping kids safe these days, you must do your research before sending that deposit off and packing up your child's sunscreen.

FARE (Food Allergy Resources and Education) has a list of allergy-friendly summer camps[2] from coast to coast. There's even a vegan option, because that's how we roll now, apparently. The great thing about camps that are already focusing on the food-allergy issue is that it's not new to them, and you should be able to trust them with your allergic child. While some on the list are specifically for kids with food allergies, others are dance, sport, and traditional summer camps that are simply known for their great accommodations.

As I mentioned earlier in the book, the Wilshire Boulevard Camps in Malibu, California, have a fabulous allergy-educated chef and kitchen staff, and their two camps of Hilltop and Hess Kramer can accommodate allergic campers and soothe parents' fears. You want to look for that perfect combo when you're talking to the people running the summer camp you're entrusting your child to for 2, 4, 6, or more weeks of his life. So be sure to ask the following questions.

- Is the kitchen staff educated on the eight main allergens (or yours, specifically), and how to prepare food safely?

- Is there a separate area of the kitchen for allergen-free food preparation?

- Is there a separate serving area, or a safe protocol, to keep the allergen-free food safe after it is prepared?

- Are there safeguards in place to identify food with, or without, allergens? What do they look like?

- Is there a nurse or other staff member on-site at all times to be able to provide medical help in the event of an emergency?

It's not easy to let our young kids out of our sight, even if they're not battling a severe food allergy, so this is a big step. If you, or your child, are not ready to take off to summer camp, don't force it. Take it from the woman who had to pick up her child from summer camp even though the policy was that never, ever, ever, happened. It's not a good experience for anyone if you're not prepared and ready.

Over the River and through the Woods

Sending the kids to stay with the grandparents is also an incredibly appealing option. Especially during those weeks of summer break when your workload just got a lot heavier and the day camp options suddenly dried up. Only you know how much you can trust your parents, or your significant other's parents, with the health of your kids, but may I suggest that you buy them a copy of this book to read? Or, if they're more of the "cursing is the devil's work" kind of memaw and pawpaw, maybe use a Sharpie on a few pages before you send it over. And pack a backpackful of safe snacks to give the family a big ol' hint of what's cool for your kid to eat.

The point being, just because your child is related to someone does not mean that someone fully understands the importance of safely prepared food. Relatives need reminders, even if it's incredibly annoying to be told what to do by the kid you raised, whose butt you wiped countless times, whose middle school shenanigans made you certain she would never be responsible enough to own a cat, much less have a baby, back in the days when no one was allergic to anything.

Acknowledgments

For all of the parents out there who are just trying to get through the day without anything catastrophic happening, thank you for reading this book and being awesome. I'm with you, and I know you're tired.

Mad props, as always, go to my agent and mom of an allergic kid, Alison Fargis at Stonesong, and her amazing team.

Jen Levesque at Rodale is not only a fantastic editor but also someone who gets my thing and has for a long time. She rocks, as do Dervla Kelly, Jean Lee, Anna Cooperberg, Marilyn Hauptly, Carol Angstadt, and the rest of the Rodale team that I'm a little bit in love with right now.

Maura Wall Hernandez again bailed me out by creating some seriously delicious recipes (those ice pops, though) and being an incredible talent and friend.

To every waiter, chef, hostess, server, person who brings me food—thank you to those of you who may be annoyed but don't make me feel like an asshole AND serve me safe food. I wish I knew who you were before I left the restaurant, but alas, I have a 15- to 30-minute waiting period post-meal. I suppose I could come back and thank you after, but that would just be weird.

To my beautiful readers over at *Gluten Is My Bitch*. Thank you for the hard-core support and continuing with me on this ridiculous journey of food deprivation. Never change! Unless that change allows you to eat whatever you want.

For help with research, testing, telling me whom to call for what, asking if I'm okay while in the throes of my deadline, the following crew rocks, hard: Chef John Bard, Catherine Crawford, Kara Dean, Cary Fagan, Victoria Harmer, Rebecca Woolf, Rebecca Coleman, Susan Matloff, Angie Tepper,

Myra Model, Fish Twins, Karly Gilbert, Aaron Flores, Nancee Jaffe, Katie Hurley, Laura Clark, Madeline Holler, Angelica Lai, Ellen, Amy, and the rest of the Goldman clan, my pops, my big brother, and the rest of the Reeves/Pevetos/Peveteauxs out there. And as always, lifelong thanks to my mom, who taught me to kick ass and take names (in the most polite Great Plainsian way), whom I miss every day.

The biggest thanks goes out to my husband, Aaron, who keeps it together when I'm on the verge, and our amazing kids, Esmé and Judah, who keep me laughing, sometimes screaming, but always amazed.

Thanks a million!

Appendix 1

Food, Glorious Food!

Whether it's finding the perfect gluten-free flour or a soy-free packaged snack, here is a list to get you started. Please note that recipes do change, so always check the label or call the manufacturer if you are in doubt of its continued safety for your kiddo. In fact, there are plenty of horror stories out there of a company changing a formula and an allergic reaction ensuing. Please read that label every time you pick it up, just to make sure it's all good. This information is accurate at the time of my research, but could have changed by the time you've picked up this book and dug into the snacks.

If you can't find these items at your local Whole Foods/New Seasons/Erewhon/Sprouts/hippie store, try online stores as well. Amazon is a great option, but so are specialty online food stores such as Direct Eats, Thrive, Swanson Health Products, and the actual brand sites of many products listed below.

For the severely allergic, I suggest you head on over to Allergence (allergence.snacksafely.com), where they work in tandem with food manufacturers to determine what foods are safe for what allergy types. Even though we finally have labeling laws in the United States, what does not have to be labeled is if the food was processed alongside another food that DOES contain the allergen your kid has to avoid at all costs. So, if you're in that camp, check out Allergence, and be 100 percent safe with packaged foods.

Favorite Eight Main Allergen-Free Easy Snacks

Stock up on these packaged and natural snacks if you have multiple allergies in your house, or among your kids' friends. Especially stock up on these if you find yourself responsible for bringing the snack to every T-ball game. You'll have safe stuff on hand for every kid hanging around.

All fruit (in its natural form)

All-natural applesauce

All vegetables (in their natural form)

Annie's Homegrown Organic Bunny Fruit Snacks

Arrowhead Mills Organic Coconut Rice & Shine hot cereal

Cybele's Free-to-Eat cookies

Enjoy Life Eat Freely snacks

Luigi's Real Italian ice

No Whey! snacks

Plain popcorn

Rice Chex, Corn Chex, Chex Clusters, Cinnamon Chex, Vanilla Chex

Sweet Alexis Bakery treats

Tasty Brand organic fruit gummy snacks

The Big Food List

If you just need to watch one or two allergens, here's a list of options you can use to bake with, eat alone, or pair with something else delicious. Use the key after each product to see what it's missing.

Key

Gluten (G), Dairy (D), Peanuts (P), Tree Nuts (TN), Soy (S), Egg (E), Fish (F), and Shellfish (SF)—means it is free of these allergens.

Again, be sure to check the labels as ingredients can, and do, change.

FLOURS/BAKING PRODUCTS

Arrowhead Mills gluten-free steel cut oats G, D, P, TN, S, E, F, SF

Authentic Foods Steve's gluten-free flour blend G, D, P, TN, S, E, F, SF

Authentic Foods Steve's gluten-free cake flour G, D, P, TN, S, E, F, SF

Better Batter all-purpose gluten-free flour G, D, P, TN, S, E, F, SF

Bob's Red Mill almond meal G, D, P, S, E, F, SF

Bob's Red Mill 1-to-1 baking gluten-free flour G, D, P, TN, S, E, F, SF (made in facility that processes tree nuts and soy)

Bob's Red Mill baking soda and baking powder G, D, P, TN, S, E, F, SF (made in facility that processes tree nuts and soy)

Bob's Red Mill gluten-free rolled oats G, D, P, TN, S, E, F, SF (made in facility that processes tree nuts and soy)

Bob's Red Mill gluten-free steel cut oats G, D, P, TN, S, E, F, SF (made in facility that processes tree nuts and soy)

Cup4Cup multi-purpose gluten-free flour G, P, TN, S, E, F, SF

Cup4Cup wholesome flour blend G, D, P, TN, S, E, F, SF

Enjoy Life all-purpose flour G, D, P, TN, S, E, F, SF

Glutino all-purpose gluten-free flour G, D, P, TN, E, F, SF

King Arthur all-purpose gluten-free flour G, D, P, TN, S, E, F, SF

Kinnikinnick panko-style breadcrumbs G, D, P, TN, S, F, SF (made in facility that processes soy)

Namaste Raw Goods quinoa flour G, D, P, TN, S, E, F, SF

Pillsbury all-purpose gluten-free flour G, D, P, TN, S, E, F, SF

Pamela's Artisan Blend gluten-free flour G, D, P, TN, S, E, F, SF

Silvana's Kitchen gluten-free multi-purpose flour G, D, P, TN, S, E, F, SF

Suzanne's Ricemellow Creme G, D, P, TN, E, F, SF

Theo dark chocolate baking bar G, D, P, TN, S, E, F, SF (manufactured on shared equipment, not suitable for severe allergies)

Trader Joe's baking soda G, D, P, TN, S, E, F, SF

FATS/OILS

Crisco butter-flavored vegetable shortening G, D, P, TN, E, F, SF

Earth Balance Buttery Sticks G, D, P, TN, E, F, SF

Earth Balance soy-free spread G, D, P, TN, S, E, F, SF

Olivado avocado oil G, D, P, TN, S, E, F, SF

Omega oil G, D, P, TN, S, E, F, SF

Spectrum organic canola oil G, D, P, TN, S, E, F, SF

Spectrum organic olive oil G, D, P, TN, S, E, F, SF

Spectrum vegetable shortening G, D, P, TN, S, E, F, SF

Spectrum virgin coconut oil G, D, P, TN, S, E, F, SF (made in facility that processes peanuts)

SWEETS/SNACKS

Amy's Andy's Dandy Candy Bars G, P, E, F, SF

BaKol Vegan Jel Dessert G, D, P, TN, S, E, F, SF

Bitsy's Brainfood Cheddar Chia Veggie Crackers D, P, TN, S, E, F, SF

Crunchmaster Popped Edamame Chips G, D, P, TN, E, F, SF

Crunchmaster Toasted Sesame Baked Rice Crackers G, D, P, TN, S, E, F, SF

Crunchmaster Multi-Seed Crackers G, D, P, TN, E, F, SF

Daiya Cheese Shreds (Pepperjack, Mozzarella, Cheddar, and Classic) G, D, P, TN, S, E, F, SF

Daiya cheese blocks and slices G, D, P, TN, S, E, F, SF

Daiya cream cheese G, D, P, TN, S, E, F, SF

Dove dark chocolate bars G, D, P, TN, E, F, SF

Dare Breton Crackers, White Bean with Salt and Pepper G, P, TN, E, F, SF

Endangered Species Dark Chocolate Bug Bites G, D, P, TN, E, F, SF

Enjoy Life Ricemilk Crunch Bar G, D, P, TN, S, E, F, SF

Enjoy Life chewy bars G, D, P, TN, S, E, F, SF

Enjoy Life Decadence Bars G, D, P, TN, S, E, F, SF

Enjoy Life Plentils Chips G, D, P, TN, S, E, F, SF

Evol Street Tacos, Shredded Chicken and Caramelized Onion G, D, P, TN, S, E, F, SF

Fancypants Baking Company cookies P, TN, F, SF

Follow Your Heart cheese slices (Provolone, American, Mozzarella, Garden Herb) D, P, TN, S, E, F, SF

The GFB bars G, D, S, E, F, SF

Glutino Original Bagel Chips G, D, P, TN, S, F, SF

Glutino Pretzel Twists G, D, P, TN, S, E, F, SF

Glutino Toaster Pastries (Apple Cinnamon and Strawberry) G, D, P, TN, S, F, SF

Hampton Creek Just Cookie Dough, Chocolate Chip D, P, TN, S, E, F, SF

Hippie Butter Gourmet Hemp Seed Butter G, D, P, TN, S, E, F, SF

Jell-O gelatin G, D, P, TN, S, E, F, SF

Kinnikinnick KinniKritter Graham Style Animal Cookies G, D, P, TN, S, E, F, SF (made in facility that processes egg yolks)

Mediterranean Snacks Sea Salt Lentil Crackers G, P, TN, S, E, F, SF (made in facility that processes egg yolks)

Milton's Craft Bakers gluten-free crackers G, P, TN, S, E, F, SF

Mrs. May's Naturals Trio Bars G, D, S, E, F, SF

Pirate's Booty Aged Cheddar Puffs G, P, TN, S, E, F, SF

Pirate's Booty Veggie Puffs G, D, P, TN, E, F, SF

Pirate's Booty Carrot Snacks G, D, P, TN, S, E, F, SF

Pumpkin butter G, D, P, TN, S, E, F, SF

Rising Hearts bagels G, D, P, TN, S, E, F, SF

Schär Honeygrams G, D, P, TN, E, F, SF

Skeeter nut-free snacks P, TN, F, SF

Skinny Crisps, all flavors G, D, P, S, E, F, SF

So Delicious almond milk G, D, P, S, E, F, SF

So Delicious cashew ice cream (varies, but all D)

So Delicious cashew milk G, D, P, S, E, F, SF

So Delicious coconut ice cream (varies, but all D)

So Delicious coconut milk G, D, P, TN, S, E, F, SF

So Delicious soy ice cream (varies, but all D)

Udi's Soft & Chewy Snickerdoodle Cookies G, P, TN, S, F, SF

Van's Say Cheese! Crackers G, P, TN, S, E, F, SF

Yehuda gluten-free matzo meal G, D, P, TN, S, F, SF

EASTER/HALLOWEEN/PIÑATA CANDY

If you check out Natural Candy Store (naturalcandystore.com), you'll go a long way in filling up the kids' Halloween bags and Easter baskets. You can search by allergen, which is how I found some of these terrific treats right here.

Annie's Homegrown Organic Bunny Fruit Snacks G, D, P, TN, S, E, F, SF

CleanCandy Root Beer Float candy G, D, P, TN, S, E, F, SF

Color Kitchen plant-based Easter egg coloring kit G, D, P, TN, S, E, F, SF

Enjoy Life chocolate bars G, D, P, TN, S, E, F, SF

Gimbal's Gourmet Jelly Beans G, D, P, TN, S, E, F, SF

Glee gum G, D, P, TN, S, E, F, SF

No Cow chocolate bunnies G, D, P, TN, S, E, F, SF

No Cow Halloween chocolates G, D, P, TN, S, E, F, SF

Peeps G, D, P, TN, S, E, F, SF

Premium Chocolatiers Benny the Milkless Bunny G, D, P, TN, E, F, SF

Premium Chocolatiers Chocolate Coffins G, D, P, TN, E, F, SF

Premium Chocolatiers Cream Veggs G, D, P, TN, E, F, SF

Spangler Dum-Dum Pops G, D, P, TN, S, E, F, SF

Strawberry Hill Jack-o-Lantern Lollipop G, D, P, TN, S, E, F, SF

Sunbursts G, P, TN, E, F, SF

Surf Sweets gummy candy G, D, P, TN, S, E, F, SF

Tootsie Pops G, P, TN, F, SF

Tootsie Rolls G, P, TN, F, SF

VerMints Pastilles G, D, P, TN, S, E, F, SF

Yummy Earth Organic Pops G, D, P, TN, S, E, F, SF

SAUCES/DRESSINGS/COOK'S HELPERS

Annie's Naturals BBQ Sauce G, D, P, TN, E, F, SF

Annie's Naturals organic ketchup G, D, P, TN, S, E, F, SF

Annie's Naturals organic mustards (Original, Dijon, Honey, Horseradish) G, D, P, TN, S, E, F, SF

Bone Suckin' Sauce G, D, P, TN, S, E, F, SF

Ener-G breadcrumbs G, D, P, TN, S, E, F, SF

Follow Your Heart Soy-Free Veganaise G, D, P, TN, S, E, F, SF

French's mustards (Spicy Brown, Honey, Dijon, Honey Dijon, Horseradish, Honey Mustard Dipping Sauce) G, D, P, TN, S, E, F, SF

Glutino breadcrumbs G, D, P, TN, S, E, F, SF

Hampton Creek Just Mayo G, D, P, TN, S, E, F, SF

Hatch Red Enchilada Sauce G, D, P, TN, E, F, SF

Heinz tomato ketchup G, D, P, TN, S, E, F, SF

Heinz yellow mustard G, D, P, TN, S, E, F, SF

Maruso soy sauce G, D, P, TN, E, F, SF

Muir Glen ketchup G, D, P, TN, S, E, F, SF

San-J Gluten-Free Tamari G, D, P, TN, E, F, SF

Schär croutons G, D, P, TN, S, E, F, SF

Spectrum light canola mayonnaise G, D, P, TN, E, F, SF

Stubb's All-Natural Bar-B-Q Sauce (all flavors except Honey Pecan) G, D, P, TN, S, E, F, SF

Stubb's marinades G, D, P, TN, E, F, SF (Texas Steakhouse flavor is eight allergen-free)

Trader Joe's gluten-free chicken, beef, and vegetable broth G, D, P, TN, S, E, F, SF

Victoria's Garden Grown organic dressings (all flavors except Carrot Ginger) G, D, P, TN, S, E, F, SF

Wright's Liquid Smoke, Hickory G, D, P, TN, S, E, F, SF

BREAKFAST CEREALS/TREATS

Bob's Red Mill Honey Oat Granola G, D, P, TN, S, E, F, SF (made in facility that also processes tree nuts and soy)

Bob's Red Mill Mighty Tasty Hot Cereal G, D, P, TN, S, E, F, SF (made in facility that also processes tree nuts and soy)

Cocomama Quinoa Cereal (Orange-Cranberry Muffin, Blueberry Pancake) G, D, P, TN, S, E, F, SF

Cream of Rice G, D, P, TN, S, E, F, SF

Enjoy Life pancake and waffle mix G, D, P, TN, S, E, F, SF

Erewhon Corn Flakes G, D, P, TN, S, E, F, SF

Erewhon Crispy Brown Rice Cereal G, D, P, TN, S, E, F, SF

Erewhon Rice Twice Cereal G, D, P, TN, S, E, F, SF

General Mills Cheerios G, D, P, TN, S, E, F, SF

General Mills Lucky Charms G, D, P, TN, S, E, F, SF

General Mills Rice and Corn Chex G, D, P, TN, E, F, SF

Glutenfreeda Blueberries, Strawberries, Brown Sugar Instant Oatmeal Cups G, D, P, TN, S, E, F, SF

Glutino Fluffy Pancake Mix G, P, TN, E, F, SF

GoGo Quinoa Pancake Mix G, D, P, TN, S, E, F, SF

GoGo Quinoa Quinoa Flakes G, D, P, TN, S, E, F, SF

KIND granola G, D, P, TN, S, E, F, SF (made in facility that processes peanuts, tree nuts, soy, and sesame seeds)

Kinnikinnick Gluten-Free Soft Donuts G, D, P, TN, S, F, SF

Nature's Path Envirokids Lightly Frosted Amazon Flakes G, D, P, TN, S, E, F, SF (made in facility that processes peanuts, tree nuts, soy)

Nature's Path EnviroKids Corn Puffs Gorilla Munch G, D, P, TN, S, E, F, SF (made in facility that processes peanuts, tree nuts, and soy)

Nature's Path Gluten-Free Organic Whole O's G, D, P, TN, S, E, F, SF (made in facility that processes peanuts, tree nuts, and soy)

Nature's Path Organic Chocolate Koala Crisp G, D, P, TN, S, E, F, SF (made in facility that processes peanuts, tree nuts, soy)

Nature's Path Organic Crispy Rice G, D, P, TN, S, E, F, SF (made in facility that processes peanuts, tree nuts, and soy)

The Pure Pantry Organic Buckwheat Flax Pancake and Baking Mix G, D, P, TN, S, E, F, SF

Purely Elizabeth Ancient Grain Granola G, D, P, TN, S, E, F, SF (made in facility that processes tree nuts and soy)

Silvana's Kitchen gluten-free pancake, waffle, and biscuit mix G, D, P, TN, S, E, F, SF

XO Baking Co. Pancake and Waffle Mix G, D, P, TN, S, E, F, SF

OTHER BAKED GOOD MIXES

Bob's Red Mill Gluten-Free Pie Crust Mix G, D, P, TN, S, E, F, SF (made in facility that processes tree nuts and soy)

Bob's Red Mill Gluten-Free Pizza Crust Mix G, D, P, TN, S, E, F, SF (made in facility that processes tree nuts and soy)

Bob's Red Mill Gluten Free Shortbread Cookie Mix G, D, P, TN, S, E, F, SF (made in facility that processes tree nuts and soy)

Enjoy Life brownie mix G, D, P, TN, S, E, F, SF

Enjoy Life muffin mix G, D, P, TN, S, E, F, SF

GoGo Quinoa Dark Chocolate Cake Mix G, D, P, TN, S, E, F, SF

King Arthur's gluten-free muffin mix G, D, P, TN, S, E, F, SF

Pamela's frosting mix (vanilla, chocolate, and salted caramel flavors) G, D, P, TN, S, E, F, SF (made in facility that processes tree nuts, soy, eggs, and milk)

The Pure Pantry Whole-Grain Dark Chocolate Cake Mix G, D, P, TN, S, E, F, SF

Schär Classic White Bread Mix G, D, P, TN, S, E, F, SF

XO Baking Co. cake mix (chocolate and vanilla flavors) G, D, P, TN, S, E, F, SF

XO Baking Co. frosting mix (vanilla and chocolate flavors) G, D, P, TN, S, E, F, SF

XO Baking Co. Pound Cake Mix G, D, P, TN, S, E, F, SF

XO Baking Co. Sugar Cookie Mix G, D, P, TN, S, E, F, SF

BREADS/WRAPS

Against the Grain pita bread G, P, TN, S, E, F, SF

Brazi Bites Brazilian Cheese Bread G, P, TN, S, F, SF

Canyon Bakehouse Everything Bagels G, D, P, TN, S, F, SF

Canyon Bakehouse Rosemary & Thyme Focaccia G, D, P, TN, S, F, SF

Glutino multigrain bread G, D, P, TN, S, F, SF (may contain soy and sesame)

LaBrea Bakery Gluten-Free White Artisan Sliced Sandwich Bread G, D, P, TN, S, F, SF

Potapas tortillas G, D, P, TN, S, E, F, SF

Rising Hearts bagels G, D, P, TN, S, E, F, SF

Rising Hearts baguettes G, D, P, TN, S, E, F, SF

Rising Hearts hot dog and hamburger buns G, D, P, TN, S, E, F, SF

Schär Parbaked Ciabatta G, D, P, TN, E, F, SF

Schär Sub Sandwich Rolls G, D, P, TN, S, E, F, SF

Trader Joe's taco shells G, D, P, TN, S, E, F, SF

Udi's Seeded Dinner Rolls G, D, P, TN, S, F, SF

Udi's Soft & Wholesome Tortillas G, D, P, TN, S, F, SF

Udi's Whole Grain Hamburger & Hot Dog Buns G, D, P, TN, S, F, SF

Whole Foods gluten-free pie crust G, P, TN, S, F, SF

PASTA

Ancient Harvest organic quinoa pasta G, D, P, TN, S, E, F, SF

Andean Dream quinoa pasta G, D, P, TN, S, E, F, SF

Annie's Homegrown Organic Vegan Mac & Cheese D, P, TN, S, E, F, SF (made in facility that processes milk, soy, and coconut)

DeBoles rice pasta G, D, P, TN, S, E, F, SF

DeBoles Artichoke Flour Pasta D, P, TN, S, E, F, SF

GoGo Quinoa macaroni G, D, P, TN, S, E, F, SF

Jovial brown rice pasta G, D, P, TN, S, E, F, SF (made in facility that processes soy)

Le Veneziane pasta G, D, P, TN, S, E, F, SF

Lundberg brown rice G, D, P, TN, S, E, F, SF

Manini's pasta (except ravioli) G, D, P, TN, S, E, F, SF

Schär Bontà d'Italia penne, fusilli, and spaghetti G, D, P, TN, S, E, F, SF

PIZZA

If you're a person living in America, you know that pizza is basically the best kid food (and let's be honest, adult as well) that you can ever have. Pizza is also traditionally filled with allergens. From gluten, to dairy, to eggs, and—if you're an anchovy freak—you have the fish thing, too. I like to be realistic about allergy-friendly pizza, and most of these don't cover all of the allergens, because if they did, they would suck. I will tell you the best allergen-free pizza option, which isn't actually pizza, but everyone in my family loves: Get a gluten-, dairy-, and egg-free crust, brush olive oil on top, add a za'tar spice, and bake on 350°F for 10 to 12 minutes until edges are crisp. So good, and eight allergen-free.

Do this if you can't find Za'atar in a store: Combine 1 tablespoon fresh oregano, 1 tablespoon ground cumin, 1 tablespoon sumac, 1 tablespoon sesame seeds, 1 tablespoon freshly ground black pepper, and 1 tablespoon sea salt. Be sure you use plenty of olive oil when you paste it onto the pizza to brown well.

For other random allergies, try these pizzas!

Against the Grain Gourmet G, P, TN, S, E, F, SF

Amy's Single-Serve Non-Dairy Rice Crust Cheeze Pizza G, D, P, TN, S, E, F, SF

Enjoy Life pizza crust mix G, D, P, TN, S, E, F, SF

LUNCHMEATS

Other than pizza, sandwiches are the next most favorite family food in America. The problem is, when your kid has allergies, figuring out how to keep the gluten, the casein, the dairy, and whatever the heck else is going on out of his lunch. So here are some picnic suggestions. Another note: When you head to your local deli, have a conversation with the guy who slices everything up. He'll probably have some great advice for those of us who are looking to make sure we have all meat, all the time.

If You're a Hot Dogger

Applegate Farms (except the Spinach & Feta version) G, D, P, TN, S, E, F, SF

Boar's Head Natural Casing G, D, P, TN, S, E, F, SF

Dietz & Watson Original Beef Franks G, D, P, TN, S, E, F, SF

Hebrew National Beef Franks G, D, P, TN, S, E, F, SF

Just Make Me a Sandwich

Applegate Farms (Black Forest Ham, Smoked Turkey Breast, Roast Beef, Roasted Chicken Breast) G, D, P, TN, S, E, F, SF

Boar's Head (Salami, Oven Roast Beef, Turkey, Applewood Smoked Uncured Ham, Seasoned Roasted Turkey Breast) G, D, P, TN, S, E, F, SF

Dietz & Watson (Oven Roasted Turkey Breast, Angus Roast Beef, Uncured Maple & Honey Ham) G, D, P, TN, S, E, F, SF

RELIGIOUS OPTIONS

There are several companies that make foods that are kosher for Passover, so check them out, if you want to. Ener-G also makes allergen-free communion wafers.

Appendix 2

Dining Out with an Allergy

You know that you're taking a risk when you go into a restaurant that has allergens present. If you have a child with a severe allergy, you may not want to risk it at all, unless the restaurant clearly states that the allergen is not at all present (like vegan restaurants where you can rest assured there is no dairy). These are restaurants that, at the very least, have a menu that accommodates some diners with food allergies. Also, recipes change, so you'll need to check it out before your heart is set on that gluten- and dairy-free pizza. No matter what your allergy is, you still need to call before you head out to make sure that your child will be accommodated, and ask the necessary questions to make sure that your child will be safe. Those questions are: Do you prepare the allergy-safe food on the same surfaces as the food with allergens? Is the allergy-safe food stored with the allergen? Is there any point at which the allergy-free food comes into contact with the allergen? At all? Seriously? Please note that you'll need to go over this again once you are inside the restaurant, because the guy answering the phone will probably not be the same person serving your food. It's a pain in the butt to go to restaurants, but sometimes, you have no choice. Or, you simply would rather skip dish duty for at least one night.

CHAIN RESTAURANTS WITH ALLERGY-FREE OPTIONS

Abuelo's

Amici Trattoria

Amy's Ice Creams

BJ's Restaurant and Brewhouse

Baja Fresh

Braum's

Buca di Beppo

Buddha's Belly

Burger Lounge

Burton's Grill & Bar

California Pizza Kitchen

Carrabba's Italian Grill

The Cheesecake Factory

Chevy's Fresh Mex

Chili's

Chipotle

Chuck E. Cheese's

Claim Jumper

The Counter

Cracker Barrel

Crust Gourmet Pizza Bar

Dave & Buster's

Don Pablo's Mexican Kitchen

El Pollo Loco

Fleming's Prime Steakhouse and Wine Bar

Freebird's World Burrito

Fresh Brothers

Garlic Jim's Famous Gourmet Pizza

The Habit Burger Grill

Houston's Restaurant

In-N-Out Burger

Islands Fine Burgers and Drinks

Jason's Deli

Joe's American Bar & Grill

Johnny Rockets

Kindkreme

Legal Sea Foods

Logan's Roadhouse

¡Lotería! Grill

Maggiano's Little Italy

Maudie's Tex-Mex

Mellow Mushroom

Mendocino Farms Sandwich Market

The Melting Pot

My Fit Foods

Not Your Average Joe's Kitchen & Bar

Qdoba Mexican Eats

The Old Spaghetti Factory

Olive Garden

On the Border Mexican Grill & Cantina

Outback Steakhouse

P. F. Chang's China Bistro

P. Terry's Burger Stand

Palomino Restaurant & Bar

Pei Wei Asian Diner

Pitfire Pizza

Pizza Hut

PizzaRev

Rainforest Cafe

Red Robin Gourmet Burgers
and Brews

Romano's Macaroni Grill

ShopHouse Southeast Asian
Kitchen

Taco Cabana

Texas Land & Cattle

ThunderCloud Subs

True Food Kitchen

Uno Chicago Grill

Veggie Grill

Wood Ranch BBQ & Grill

Yard House

zpizza

Zankou Chicken

Appendix 3

Best Responses to Jerks

Although not normally in such a book (but then again it is not your normal allergy guide), this is the section you resort to when someone says, "Surely one bite won't kill him."

"Whatever happens to him is going to happen to you." (said while cracking your knuckles)

"And a little bit of not being an asshole won't kill you."

"Sorry, I didn't recognize you outside of the hospital without your scrubs on."

"Assholesaywhat?" (said quickly, while looking expectantly for a response, which should be "What?" Yes, I'm in 7th grade.)

"Oh, right. You're the expert, and I'm just an overprotective mom who has lived in terror of losing her child for the past 8 years. Surely, I should listen to you." (bat eyelashes adorably)

Resources

You're so ready now to tackle food allergies head-on that you probably don't even need these resources. But, hey, I worked so hard to find snacks, baking supplies, restaurants, blogs, organizations, and smart people who can also help you out, now you have to look! During my research, I noticed something surprising. While I could find so many gluten-free, vegan (which means dairy-free and egg-free), and heart-healthy (low-fat, low-sodium) menus at restaurants and products in stores, searching for the other allergens turned up a fraction of the results. At first, I thought it was because my gluten-free eye has been trained so intensely for the past 5 years, and then I realized that the gluten-free trend people talk about so much is totally a thing. I know. I'm slow.

I found it shocking that foods that can cause anaphylaxis and death came with fewer warning labels than those with gluten and wheat (which can also cause anaphylaxis, but wheat is not as common as an allergen that can result in anaphylaxis). I was floored. Again, since I'm slow, it took me awhile to realize that the reason my own problem was satisfied with so many more options is simply because no one goes on a peanut-free diet to lose weight and become a tennis star. This is the struggle for the food allergic. A true food problem— a life-threatening food problem—is not taken as seriously as a fad diet. All the more reason to raise our voices, demand more choices, and advocate for our kids. Sure, I benefit from the gluten-free trend as a person who has a real disease that can (eventually) lead to death, if not controlled. But the day celebs drop their gluten-free diets for the next biggest thing, I'll also be searching for a gluten-free menu and reminiscing about the "good old days" when everyone was scared of gluten.

Still, there are some fantastic people out there making foods free of all of the eight main allergens, and sometimes even more! Let's talk about them right now instead of dwelling on the unfairness of life.

Some of you will be able to grab these allergy-friendly items at your local store; others will search high and low for what just became your child's favorite gluten-free cereal. If you cannot find it locally, remember the Internet is your friend. From Amazon or Thrive Market to Vitacost and the companies producing the products themselves, you'll be able to get your hands on the good stuff.

Have fun exploring, and remember that recipes, restaurants, and websites do change, and this information was the most up-to-date at the time of publication. Good luck, and stay safe!

Allergy-Friendly Magazines

There are some fantastic periodicals that you can subscribe to or check out online to stay up-to-date on all of the latest in allergen-free news, while enjoying new recipes and stories from people who are living the lifestyle.

Allergic Living (allergicliving.com)

Delight Gluten Free Magazine (delightglutenfree.com)

GFF Magazine (gffmag.com)

Gluten Free & More (formerly *Living Without* magazine) (glutenfreeandmore.com)

Simply Gluten Free Magazine (simplygluten-free.com)

My Favorite Allergy-Friendly Cookbooks and Guides

Allergic Girl: Adventures in Living Well with Food Allergies by Sloane Miller. This is a fun read, which says a lot when you're talking about living with multiple food allergies. Miller has learned how to navigate the world with multiple food allergies and has loads of advice on living with food in a positive way, even when it can be a roadblock to your health.

Allergy-Free and Easy Cooking: 30-Minute Meals without Gluten, Wheat, Dairy, Eggs, Soy, Peanuts, Tree Nuts, Fish, Shellfish, and Sesame by Cybele Pascal. The woman behind the cookies, Pascal offers up delicious recipes with a side of advice.

The Allergy-Free Pantry: Make Your Own Staples, Snacks, and More without Wheat, Gluten, Dairy, Eggs, Soy, or Nuts by Colette Martin. When Martin's son was diagnosed with multiple food allergies, she had to forget what she knew about baking and go to town with wheat-, dairy-, egg-, soy-, and nut-free meals and snacks instead. In other words, she's an incredibly creative lady who knows her stuff.

The Complete Guide to Living Well Gluten-Free: Everything You Need to Know to Go from Surviving to Thriving by Beth Hillson. She's not joking when she calls this the complete guide. Buy this book, and you'll use it as a reference tool for everything from picking a physician to getting over getting glutened.

Don't Kill the Birthday Girl: Tales from an Allergic Life by Sandra Beasley. This is a dark, funny romp through the life of a girl who has every allergy you can possibly think of and more. Honeydew allergy, anyone? I like to go back to Beasley's book when I'm feeling overwhelmed with just my one food issue. It will make you feel like you absolutely have your own food situation under control.

The Essential Gluten-Free Restaurant Guide by Triumph Dining. An excellent resource in print or online, these are the people who bring you the "I'm gluten-free" cards in every language.

The Everyday Art of Gluten-Free: 125 Savory and Sweet Recipes Using 6 Fail-Proof Flour Blends by Karen Morgan. The lady behind Austin's Blackbird Bakery, Morgan has a way with pastry. You'll want this book if only for the "donut" flour blend. Your kids will thank you.

The Food Allergy Mama's Fast, Easy Family Meals: Dairy, Egg, and Nut Free Recipes for Every Day and *The Food Allergy Mama's Baking Book:*

Great Dairy-, Egg-, and Nut-Free Treats for the Whole Family by Kelly Rudnicki. I know Rudnicki and have seen her boundless energy in action. Which is why she quickly became the preeminent mom expert in food allergies after one of her sons was diagnosed with a severe dairy allergy. This lady cooks, writes, and raises five kids while being a food-allergy warrior. Yes, she kicks ass, and you want her on your side.

The Gluten-Free Table: The Lagasse Girls Share Their Favorite Meals by Jilly Lagasse and Jessie Lagasse Swanson. Yep, it's those Lagasse girls, and having a professional chef for a dad has absolutely helped these ladies out when they had to go G-free. In addition to creating mouthwatering, gluten-free recipes, these sisters are adorable, and you can't help being charmed by them.

Gluten Freedom: The Nation's Leading Expert Offers the Essential Guide to a Healthy, Gluten-Free Lifestyle by Alessio Fasano, MD, with Susie Flaherty. The preeminent expert on celiac disease, treatment, and the future of gluten-free, Dr. Fasano explains it all to those of us living with the pain of not being able to eat croissants.

Gluten Is My Bitch: Rants, Recipes, and Ridiculousness for the Gluten-Free by April Peveteaux. That's me! Why, yes, this is my book, and that's why I think you should have it. Especially if you're feeling ranty or ridiculous or in need of some gluten-free chicken and waffles.

Go Dairy Free: The Guide and Cookbook for Milk Allergies, Lactose Intolerance, and Casein-Free Living by Alisa Marie Fleming. The most comprehensive guide to living a dairy-free life. Fleming gives the reader 225 recipes that satisfy your daily and special-occasion needs. also a guide to living dairy-free. Fleming discusses how to maintain your health while losing this source of vitamins and minerals.

The How Can It Be Gluten-Free Cookbook by the editors at America's Test Kitchen. The experts at the Test Kitchen have perfected a variety of gluten-free breads and many other recipes. You can always trust a cookbook from

America's Test Kitchen, and it's beyond exciting that they went gluten-free. Even better than one gluten-free cookbook, ATK has produced two at the time of this writing.

Yummy Supper by Erin Scott is the most aspirational gluten-free cookbook, while still being completely doable. The focus on fresh, local, seasonal ingredients comes naturally to this Berkeley-based cook and photographer and I found myself dog-earing, basically, the entire book.

Books for Allergic Kids and Their Friends

Depending on the age of your allergic kiddo, she may be able to enjoy the above books and magazines. For the younger crowd, however, here are a few suggestions to help them understand what the heck is going on, and be entertained at the same time.

Allie the Allergic Elephant: A Children's Story of Peanut Allergies; Cody the Allergic Cow: A Children's Story of Milk Allergies; Chad the Allergic Chipmunk: A Children's Story of Nut Allergies, all by Nicole Smith. These stories cover peanut, milk, and tree-nut allergies, respectively, through the lives and times of these allergic animals. Smith is also a fierce advocate for those with food allergies, and has changed food labeling for the better.

The Itchy Kids Club: Silly Poems for Itchy Kids by Jill Grabowski. This is a general allergy book that includes one of the most annoying symptoms for kids—the itchiness that can drive a kindergartener crazy. Luckily, these cute poems will distract him for a moment.

The No Biggie Bunch Everyday Cool with Food Allergies by Michael Pistiner, MD, MMSc. This book is an overall education for your kids on food allergies and how to manage them in every type of situation. It's a great book to read with your kids before they start school, go on a sleepover, or go away to camp. There are other smaller *No Biggie Bunch* books for specific allergies, but this is a great guide to help empower your allergic kid.

The Princess and the Peanut Allergy by Wendy McClure. This is a great example of when your own child doesn't have a food allergy, but her friend does. McClure showcases problem-solving between kids, and how to put yourself in someone else's shoes in the most adorable manner.

Why Can't I Have a Cupcake? A Book for Children with Allergies and Food Sensitivities by Betsy Childs. This book asks the most important question every kid with food allergies has, and illustrates a like-minded community where the allergic little one won't feel alone.

Support Groups and Blogs

At some point, you're going to want to connect with other people who get what it's like to live in constant vigilance and are very tired of serving quinoa for dinner. Luckily, there are many organizations out there to support parents and kids battling food allergies. There are also some fantastic blogs out there that will make you laugh, cry, and offer a suggestion to help you make a delicious dessert without dairy. While some organizations and blogs cover the gamut, some are specific to what's going on with your kid. Reach out before you're at the end of your rope, so you have some backup when you need it.

GENERAL FOOD ALLERGIES

AllerCoach (allercoach.com)

Allergy Shmallergy (shmallergy.wordpress.com)

AllergicChild (home.allergicchild.com)

AllergyEats (allergyeats.com)

AllergyHome (allergyhome.org)

FARE—Food Allergy Research & Education (foodallergy.org)

Food Allergy Buzz (foodallergybuzz.com)

Food Allergy Mama (foodallergymama.com)

Grateful Foodie (gratefulfoodie.com)

KidsHealth (kidshealth.org)

Kids with Food Allergies (kidswithfoodallergies.org)

Learning to Eat Allergy-Free (learningtoeatallergyfree.com)

Multiple Food Allergy Help (multiplefoodallergyhelp.com)

CELIAC DISEASE/GLUTEN ALLERGIES

Beyond Celiac (celiaccentral.org)

Canadian Celiac Association (celiac.ca)

Celiac Disease Foundation (celiac.org)

Celiac Support Association (csaceliacs.org)

National Institute of Health Celiac Disease Awareness Campaign (celiac.nih.gov)

Raising Jack with Celiac (raisingjackwithceliac.com)

Raising Our Celiac Kids (celiac.com)

DAIRY ALLERGIES/LACTOSE INTOLERANCE

Go Dairy Free (godairyfree.org)

Jeanette's Healthy Living (jeanetteshealthyliving.com) (also gluten-free and vegan)

MilkFreeMom (milkfreemom.com)

The Spunky Coconut (thespunkycoconut.com)

PEANUT AND TREE-NUT ALLERGIES

Managing Peanut Allergies (peanutallergyfacts.org)

No Nuts Moms Group (nonutsmomsgroup.weebly.com)

Please Don't Pass the Nuts (allergicgirl.blogspot.com)

Conferences and Expos

FABCon

There is no reason that you shouldn't start a blog if you're dealing with a kid who has food allergies. Mostly because you'll connect with other people who have the same situation, regardless of food issues. And then, you totally get a conference! But honestly, as someone who started a blog dealing with food issues, I'm a big proponent of your doing the same and meeting amazing people. Then, you get invited to the food allergy blog conference, FABcon. WIN.

FABcon (fablogcon.com) is where you should be looking to sort out if you're taking a road trip to Phoenix or Vegas, or wherever people will embrace you and not smear any allergens on you at all. The best thing about this conference is that all the people who are talking about food allergies are there, which means all the companies who care about making things better for our kids will also be there. It really is a serious group of people who are also a load of fun. It could perhaps inspire you, the parent of an allergic kid, to start a blog. Just so you can get away for a mini-vacation. Don't tell your kids I said that.

Celiac Disease Foundation National Conference (celiac.org). This annual conference and expo attracts the best in the industry, and I've personally been attending every year since receiving my celiac diagnosis. It takes place in the Los Angeles area every year, most recently making Pasadena its home base.

GF and AF Expos (gfafexpo.com). From California to Massachusetts, with stop-offs in between, this is the largest gluten-free expo in the United States.

Gluten-Free Food Allergy Fest (glutenfreefoodallergyfest.com). The *Gluten-Free & More* (formerly *Living Without* magazine) family has branched out to host gluten-free food festivals all around the country. With hundreds of exhibitors, bloggers, and gluten-free peeps, you will eat and meet well.

There are also many local support groups, so check out your area meet-ups and offshoots of any of the above organizations, and get out there!

Endnotes

INTRODUCTION

1 https://www.foodallergy.org/facts-and-stats

2 http://www.cdc.gov/healthyschools/foodallergies/index.htm

3 http://www.wnem.com/story/23073855/parent-upset-over-school-nut-ban-loses-lawsuit

4 http://www.momnewsdaily.com/mom-sues-school-over-peanut-butter-ban/

5 http://www.scarymommy.com/over-the-top-allergy-parent-shames-neighborhood -for-their-halloween-candy-offerings/

6 This is categorically untrue.

CHAPTER 1

1 http://www.foodallergy.org/

2 http://www.foodallergy.org/file/emergency-care-plan.pdf

3 http://www.ewg.org/foodnews/dirty_dozen_list.php

CHAPTER 2

1 http://health.howstuffworks.com/diseases-conditions/allergies/food-allergy/peanut /how-many-people-die-each-year-from-peanut-allergies.htm

2 This is actually unfounded, and the author is too lazy to Google "Galapagos + food allergies."

CHAPTER 3

1 http://www.ncbi.nlm.nih.gov/pubmed/20462634

2 http://www.nejm.org/doi/full/10.1056/NEJMoa1414850

3 http://www.fda.gov/Food/GuidanceRegulation /GuidanceDocumentsRegulatoryInformation/Allergens/ucm106890.htm#q1

4 http://www.wcpo.com/news/local-news/boone-county/hebron/mom-girl-with
-celiac-disease-has-to-sit-alone-during-school-lunch

5 http://health.usnews.com/health-news/health-wellness/articles/2015/01/12
/help-my-child-is-bullied-because-of-food-allergies

CHAPTER 9

1 https://seaworldparks.com/seaworld-orlando/-/media/Allergen_Info
/AllergenChefCard.ashx

2 https://www.foodallergy.org/camps/camp-list

Recipe Categories

For the nonallergic, religious, or just plain interested, this list of recipes will tell you quickly what you can and cannot feed to your hungry special-diet crew. You can also make these supertreats and just wander around your party saying, "Oh, this is low-FODMAP, don't ya' know?" and feel like a boss.

Please note that kosher means kosher-style (refer to Chapter 4 for an explanation of kosher (style, glatt, and strict) meals. I've included recipes under the vegan section that can be made vegan with the proper substitution, as noted in the full recipes. A note on Paleo: The recipes I've included are fairly strict Paleo. If you're super into this diet, you'll find out very quickly that there are several schools of thought on Paleo, and why not? It's a made-up thing. So if you want to include Taco Pie in your Paleo diet, who am I to stop you? You do you, and do it well.

Happy picking and choosing!

Vegan (or Vegan Adaptable) Recipes

Arnold Palmer Ice Pops

Blueberry-Basil Sorbet

Chocolate Bark

Chocolate Coconut Panna Cotta (using vegan gelatin)

Coconut Cream Ice Pops

Cream-Filled Chocolate Cupcakes (using Ricemellow creme)

Cream-Filled Sponge Cakes (using Ricemellow creme)

Cupcake Bowls with Fruit Filling

Dr. Pepper Sorbet

Guacamole Pepper Bites

Hot Cocoa Cubes (with vegan chocolate)

It's a Truffle Party!

Mama's Kickin' Black Bean Dip

Mango-Pineapple Ice Pops

Mini Frozen Fruit Kabobs

Mushroom Quesadillas (with Daiya or other vegan cheese substitute)

Pie Crust

Plain Ol' Guacamole

Pom-Orange Sparkly Punch

Popcorn Balls

Raspberry-Lime Seltzer

Raspberry-Limeade Sorbet

Snickerdoodles

Sparkly Jell-O Salad (using vegan gelatin)

Spicy Vegan Cauliflower Buffalo "Wings"

Strawberry Cheesecake Ice Pops

Strawberry Lemonade Ice Pops

Sweet & Spicy Peas

Sweet & Savory Hand Pies— 3 Ways

Vegan Breakfast of Champions

Vegan "Hot Dogs"

Vegan Hot Dog Buns

Veggie Tempura

Yum Chips

Kosher Recipes

Arnold Palmer Ice Pops

Berry Yogurt Drops

Breakfast Tacos

Caramel Apples

Chicken & Quinoa Salad for the FODMAP Crowd

Chicken Satay

Chicken Tinga Taquitos

Choco-Coconut Paleo Brownies

Chocolate Bark

Chocolate Coconut Panna Cotta

Cinnamon Toaster Tarts

Coconut Cream Ice Pops

Coconut Key Lime Mousse

Cream-Filled Chocolate Cupcakes

Cream-Filled Sponge Cakes

Crunchy Cheese Crackers

Cupcake Bowls with Fruit Filling

Guacamole Pepper Bites

Hot Cocoa Cubes

It's a Truffle Party!

Lemon Bars

Mama's Kickin' Black Bean Dip

Mango-Pineapple Ice Pops

Millet Candy Crispy Bars

Mini Frozen Fruit Kabobs

Monster Cookies

Mushroom Quesadillas

My Favorite Kosher Chicken Dinner

Nut-Free Carrot Cake

Pie Crust

Plain Ol' Guacamole

Pom-Orange Sparkly Punch

Popcorn Balls

Pretzel Pups (using all-beef hot dogs)

Raspberry-Lime Seltzer

Rice Balls with Peas

Rice Chex Chicken Fingers (using rice milk)

Snickerdoodles

Sparkly Jell-O Salad

Spicy Buffalo Wings

Spicy Vegan Cauliflower Buffalo "Wings"

Strawberry Cheesecake Ice Pops

Strawberry Lemonade Ice Pops

SunButter Buckeyes

SunButter Crispy Treats

SunButter Fudge

SunButter Sundaes

Sweet & Spicy Peas

Sweet & Savory Hand Pies— 3 Ways

Vegan Breakfast of Champions

Vegan "Hot Dogs"

Vegan Hot Dog Buns

Veggie Tempura

Yum Chips

Low-FODMAP Recipes

Arnold Palmer Ice Pops

Blueberry-Basil Sorbet

Chicken & Quinoa Salad for the FODMAP Crowd

Chocolate Bark

Chocolate Coconut Panna Cotta

Coconut Cream Ice Pops

Dr. Pepper Sorbet

Mango-Pineapple Ice Pops

Popcorn Balls

Raspberry-Limeade Sorbet

Sparkly Jell-O Salad

Strawberry Cheesecake Ice Pops

Strawberry Lemonade Ice Pops

Yum Chips

Refined Sugar–Free Recipes

Arnold Palmer Ice Pops

Bacon & Tomato Soup

Breakfast Tacos

Chicken & Quinoa Salad for the FODMAP Crowd

Chicken Tinga Taquitos

Coconut Cream Ice Pops

Crunchy Cheese Crackers

Guacamole Pepper Bites

It's a Truffle Party!

Mama's Kickin' Black Bean Dip

Mango-Pineapple Ice Pops

Mini Frozen Fruit Kabobs

Mushroom Quesadillas

My Favorite Kosher Chicken Dinner

Plain Ol' Guacamole

Pretzel Pups

Raspberry-Lime Seltzer

Rice Balls with Peas

Sausage Balls

Spicy Buffalo Wings

Strawberry Cheesecake Ice Pops

Strawberry Lemonade Ice Pops

Taco Pie

Vegan "Hot Dogs"

Vegan Hot Dog Buns

Vegan Breakfast of Champions

Veggie Tempura

Yum Chips

Paleo Recipes

Bacon & Tomato Soup

Choco-Coconut Paleo Brownies

Chocolate Bark

Chocolate Coconut Panna Cotta

Guacamole Pepper Bites

My Favorite Kosher Chicken Dinner

Plain Ol' Guacamole

Spicy Buffalo Wings (if using ghee instead of butter)

Spicy Vegan Cauliflower Buffalo "Wings"

Vegan "Hot Dogs" (using coconut aminos instead of tamari)

Yum Chips

Index

Boldface page numbers indicate photographs. <u>Underscored</u> references indicate boxed text.

peanut-butter alternatives, <u>100</u>
prepared and convenience foods, 69–70
sauces, commercial, 183–84
soy, 38–39, 44
sugar, 38
tree nuts, 4, 36–37, 44

J

Jell-O
Sparkly Jell-O Salad, 153
Jelly beans
Sparkly Jell-O Salad, 153

K

Kosher, 53–54, 210–11

L

Labels
FDA requirements for, 43
on homemade treats, 109–10, 134
reading, 37, 42–44
Lemons
Arnold Palmer Ice Pops, 136
Lemon Bars, 117
Strawberry Lemonade, 159
Strawberry Lemonade Ice Pops, 135
Limes
Chicken Satay, 98
Coconut Key Lime Mousse, 119
Raspberry-Limeade Sorbet, 145

M

Mangoes
Mango-Pineapple Ice Pops, 137

Marshmallows
Creme-Filled Chocolate Cupcakes, 114–15
Creme-Filled Sponge Cakes, 112–13
Millet Candy Crispy Bars, 130
Sunbutter Crispy Treats, 100–101
Mushrooms
Mushroom Quesadillas, 95
Veggie Tempura, 152

O

Onions
Chicken Tinga Taquitos, 92–93
Orange juice
Pom-Orange Sparkly Punch, 158

P

Paleo diet, 56–57, 212–13
Party treats
beverages (*See* Beverages)
planning for, 132–34
Party treats, savory. *See also* Snacks
Guacamole Pepper Bites, 149
Mama's Kickin' Black Bean Dip, 144
Plain Ol' Guacamole, 141
Sausage Balls, 140
snack trays, <u>142–43</u>, **143**
Spicy Buffalo Wings, 150
Spicy Vegan Cauliflower Buffalo
"Wings," 151
Sweet and Spicy Peas, 156
Taco Pie, 154–55
Veggie Tempura, 152
Party treats, sweet. *See also* Bake sale
treats; Desserts; Desserts, frozen
Arnold Palmer Ice Pops, 136
Berry Yogurt Drops, 148
Blueberry-Basil Sorbet, 146

"Having a child with food allergies is challenging. Allergy moms need support to keep going and a laugh every now and then to keep from killing people. *Bake Sales Are My B*tch* is the best allergy mom book EVAH! It's funny and educational and easy for anyone to pick up and understand."

—**Leah Segedie, Mamavation.com**